# MAXIMIZING
# PARAPROFESSIONAL
# POTENTIAL

The Professional Practices in Adult Education and Human Resource Development Series explores issues and concerns of practitioners who work in the broad range of settings in adult and continuing education and human resource development.

The books are intended to provide information and strategies on how to make practice more effective for professionals and those they serve. They are written from a practical viewpoint and provide a forum for instructors, administrators, policy makers, counselors, trainers, managers, program and organizational developers, instructional designers, and other related professionals.

*Editorial correspondence should be sent to the Editor-in-Chief:*

*Michael W. Galbraith*
Florida Atlantic University
Department of Educational Leadership
College of Education
Boca Raton, FL 33431

# MAXIMIZING PARAPROFESSIONAL POTENTIAL

Joye A. Norris

Susan S. Baker

KRIEGER PUBLISHING COMPANY
MALABAR, FLORIDA
1999

Original Edition   1998

Printed and Published by
**KRIEGER PUBLISHING COMPANY**
**KRIEGER DRIVE**
**MALABAR, FLORIDA 32950**

FROM A DECLARATION OF PRINCIPLES JOINTLY ADOPTED BY A COMMITTEE OF THE AMERCAN BAR ASSOCIATION AND A COMMITTEE OF PUBLISHERS:
This publication is designed to provide accurate and authoritative information in regard to the subject matter covered. It is sold with the understanding that the publisher is not engaged in rendering legal, accounting, or other professional service. If legal advice or other expert assistance is required, the services of a competent professional person should be sought.

Library of Congress Cataloging-In-Publication Data

Norris, Joye A.
    Maximizing paraprofessional potential / Joye A. Norris, Susan S. Baker.
        p.   cm. — (The professional practices in adult education and human resource development series)
    Includes bibliographical references (p. ) and index.
    ISBN 1-57524-027-0 (alk. paper)
    1. Paraprofessionals in social service—In-service training—United States.   2. Paraprofessionals in social service—Training of—United States.   I. Baker, Susan S.   II. Title.   III. Series.
HV40.4.N67   1999
361'.0068'3—dc21                                                    98-17871
                                                                          CIP

10 9 8 7 6 5 4 3 2

# CONTENTS

# PREFACE

One hundred and fifty paraprofessional nutrition educators were gathered for their annual conference. During a morning training session, the facilitator asked them to jot down and then share with someone else two victories they had experienced in their work over the past few months. A brief sample of their anonymous responses follows:

- When I arrived at my client's home, I was astonished to see that she had cleaned off her kitchen counter without my having to help her. She is beginning to look forward to seeing me.
- I learned last week that Child Protective Services had decided not to remove my client's three-year-old son from her care. I know that I helped to make that decision possible because I helped the mother start managing her food stamps and her shopping much more effectively.
- After doing a lesson on healthy snacks, the women at our local shelter stayed an extra hour after I finished the lesson because they were so excited about learning!
- When I arrived at our local public housing development to facilitate a group lesson on infant care, for the first time ever, everyone showed up! I must be making some progress.

Who are these people? They are part of a legion of non-professional, human service workers who work every day under the most difficult circumstances and try to make a difference in their clients' lives. They are usually hired, not for their degrees or knowledge of subject matter, but for their life experiences, cultural, social, and economic backgrounds, and their ability to relate to clients. They are intimately involved with our nation's most difficult challenges, including reducing teen pregnancy, increasing child immunization rates, preventing neighborhood violence and drug activities, decreasing infant mortality, improving outcomes in high-risk pregnancies, improving the diets of limited-resource families, and caring for infants and toddlers who are developmentally delayed. These people, referred to as paraprofessionals, are recruited and brought into human service agencies with the promise that they will receive the training needed to perform what they are asked to do. The message to them is, "Give us your experiences, your desire to help, and your personal attributes, and we will teach you everything else you need." This book is about fulfilling that promise.

We have worked with human service paraprofessionals for a decade, in day-to-day supervisory capacities, as trainers, and as program administrators. As our experience grew, so did our awareness that very little existed in the way of publications to help supervisors and trainers get the most from their paraprofessionals and show excellent program outcomes. We grew to understand that training human service paraprofessionals was not business as usual where professionals train professionals. We saw it instead as a balance between facilitating the paraprofessionals' growth and development while also developing their skills.

We developed a model for training based first and foremost on our respect for human service paraprofessionals and the difficult circumstances under which they work. Even though their compensation rarely matches their worth, they perform their job because they want to make a difference. Our model provides a salute to them as well as a framework for the training and support they receive.

Our Sequential Development Model has been constructed on the assumption that those individuals responsible for training and supervising paraprofessionals are willing to make the necessary commitment, set aside the necessary time, and devote the necessary planning to develop their staff and improve program outcomes. We believe that effective training happens by design, not by default.

## Who Will Benefit from This Book?

The beneficiaries of *Maximizing Paraprofessional Potential* fall into four general categories:

1. supervisors of beginning programs who are directly responsible for the paraprofessionals;
2. managers responsible for existing programs that utilize paraprofessionals;
3. supervisors considering using paraprofessionals to deliver human services; and
4. individuals involved in adult education programs at the undergraduate and graduate school levels.

With this book the supervisor of a brand new program will discover how to get started, from hiring the right people through managing their performance. One of the authors met recently with a supervisor of paraprofessionals. "When I was hired for this position, I had no clue about how to hire the paraprofessionals, let alone train them. I was given an office, a phone, a secretary, and told to get started. It took me my first two years to get it all figured out, by trial and error, and I'm certainly still learning." (S. Lehr, personal communication, May 1, 1997). *Maximizing Paraprofessional Potential* will take new supervisors and trainers through the entire process.

Supervisors of existing programs, particularly if they have the day-to-day responsibility for the paraprofessionals, will find that this volume identifies what they *have been doing*, what they have not been doing, and what they *need to improve*. The final chapter of the book contains strategies for implementing immediate improvements with minimal changes.

Some readers may be more involved in deciding whether they want to use paraprofessionals to deliver services and promote behavior change. This volume provides what we believe is a realistic picture of what is required to effectively use paraprofessionals and to reap program outcome benefits.

Students of training and development and adult education will find that the principles and practices outlined in this book have a wide application. For instance, Vella's (1994; 1995) view of adult learning and program design, which we employ in our practice and in this book, may be applied to a much broader training arena than the one we describe. The principles and practices we have included in this volume will also be of value to trainers working in other fields, including businesses that employ nonprofessional, hourly workers.

Human service paraprofessionals typically work for public or nonprofit agencies. These agencies include Cooperative Extension Services; public health and social services departments; Head Start; Women, Infants and Children (WIC); mental health and drug prevention organizations; community action centers; education nonprofits; health clinics and hospitals; universities; and other local, state, and federal departments. Agency directors should find this volume useful, as should various outreach program coordinators.

The health insurance industry which operates health plans for low-income clients exemplifies the use of paraprofessionals in the for-profit sector. Paraprofessionals are sent out into communities to teach families about immunization, well-baby examinations, and preventive care. Administrators working with for-profit agencies will benefit from *Maximizing Paraprofessional Potential*.

In practice, the Sequential Development Model featured in this book is both overlapping and circuitous. However, each component—each chapter—will provide readers with several strategies and practices that can be immediately implemented. This book is intended to fill the gap between the decision to employ human service paraprofessionals and the skills and knowledge professionals need to train and supervise them.

# ACKNOWLEDGMENTS

The authors wish to acknowledge the support and encouragement shown by their families during the development of this volume. The authors are grateful for the editing support provided by Charles Baker and Nancy K. Evans. We also want to thank Mary Overfield for her assistance with editing and indexing. We also thank the thousands of paraprofessionals with whom we have worked, whose genuine commitment and dedication to making a difference in the lives of others have been a source of inspiration to us.

# THE AUTHORS

Joye A. Norris is an education consultant and trainer with her own company, Carolina Learning Design. She received her B.A. degree and M.S. degree in education from the University of Kentucky, and earned the Ed.D. in Counselor Education at North Carolina State University.

In recent years, Norris has focused her attention on three areas: literacy education, popular education, and paraprofessional training. She remains actively involved in each area. She was coauthor of a previous Krieger publication in this series, *Developing Literacy Programs for Homeless Adults* (1992). In addition, Joye directs the Center for Literacy Alternatives, dedicated to examining nontraditional methods of instruction. She is a master trainer with the Jubilee Popular Education Center in Raleigh, North Carolina, and regularly provides week-long intensive training programs for educators from all over the country and from international locations, as well.

Norris's interest in providing training for human service paraprofessionals and her recognition of their unique needs led to the development of this volume. Thus far, Norris has trained paraprofessionals in 17 states for Cooperative Extension Service programs, WIC programs and public health agencies. She delights in their desire to make a difference and their amazing resourcefulness.

Norris recently received the National Council for Education and Training Leadership Award for Region IV. She resides in Garner, North Carolina, and enjoys reading, kayaking, country music, camping, and gathering inspiration from frequent trips to the coast.

Susan S. Baker is the coordinator of the Expanded Food

and Nutrition Education Program (EFNEP), with the North Carolina Cooperative Extension Service, and she directs the In-Home Breastfeeding Support Program. In her nine years with North Carolina Cooperative Extension Service and North Carolina State University, she has developed, piloted, and managed innovative programs at the county and state levels utilizing paraprofessionals in the delivery of nutrition education and breastfeeding support for limited-resource audiences.

She earned her B.S. in foods and nutrition at Meredith College and her M.Ed. in adult education at North Carolina State University. Currently she is pursuing an Ed.D. in training and development at North Carolina State University. Her research interests include training and staff-development issues related to Extension nutrition paraprofessionals and the effectiveness of paraprofessional instructors in manifesting behavioral change.

Baker has authored an orientation and initial-training program for paraprofessionals who deliver nutrition education via EFNEP. She also coauthored and coordinated the development of a three-volume set of manuals (including a comprehensive curriculum and corresponding guide for implementation and management) for training paraprofessionals to become breastfeeding counselors in the widely recognized In-Home Breastfeeding Support Program.

Baker's passion for the potential of paraprofessionals, particularly with regard to staff development, led her to pursue graduate studies in training and development and to collaborate in the production of this volume. She has designed numerous, innovative educational programs for delivery by paraprofessionals, and has presented the applied research associated with these programs at national and international meetings.

She lives in Raleigh, North Carolina, and her personal interests include cooking, antiques, cinema, and enjoying family time with her husband and daughter.

# CHAPTER 1

## The Sequential Development Model for Maximizing Paraprofessional Potential

Truax and Carkhuff (1967) raised the possibility that nonprofessionals with life experiences similar to their clients' might be more effective counselors than professionals with content knowledge, but totally different backgrounds. They referred to empathy—the ability to place one's self in someone else's shoes—and the nonprofessional's ability to create a quality relationship with clients. This relationship, according to Truax and Carkhuff, was more important in working with people in crisis and bringing about positive outcomes than was theoretical and technical knowledge of subject matter. They believed that nonprofessionals were perfectly capable of creating these quality relationships.

Over the years, human service providers, looking to put a dent in the abysmal social, educational, and health outcomes associated with poverty, have turned to paraprofessionals to serve as the first line of intervention. Initially influenced by the early empathy studies, professionals have looked to nonprofessionals with socioeconomic and cultural backgrounds similar to those of the target audience to provide programs in an effort to change behavior. Additional research has shown that nonprofessionals can be very effective helpers or teachers (Olson, 1994). The Cooperative Extension Service, for example, has been employing paraprofessionals extensively for more than 25 years to deliver nutrition education. Public health departments employ outreach workers to help address a variety of problems including prenatal and immigrant health care. Community-based agencies use paraprofessionals to mentor, to provide peer counseling, and to address serious issues such as teen violence, pregnancy, and drug abuse. Private, managed-care health providers employ paraprofessionals to do community outreach work, including talking to families about the importance of well-baby checkups and immunizations. Large public hospitals are employing paraprofessionals to provide breastfeeding assistance to new mothers with limited incomes.

Many of the programs cited as examples refer to their human service nonprofessional employees as outreach workers, advisors, mentors, aides, helpers, peer counselors, and intermediaries. We are choosing the term *paraprofessional*, meaning that the person works around or closely with professional staff and at the same time extends what the professional can do. Our emphasis is on the human service paraprofessional whose socioeconomic and/or cultural background is similar to, although not necessarily the same as, the audience being served. Paraprofessionals typically are not college graduates.

One reader response at this point might be, "Why do we need a book focused on paraprofessional training? Is there not already an abundance of books and manuals on training employees? Can't we just use those?" The answer is "Yes," but only with major adaptations and a thorough understanding of the role of paraprofessionals and our role in training them. This book addresses these particular needs for the reader.

This chapter begins with a discussion of our point of view on training human service paraprofessionals and our understanding of the roles of the supervisor/trainer. The next segment describes characteristics of paraprofessionals and addresses why training should be developed specifically for them. Following the characteristics is an overview of the Sequential Development Model for maximizing paraprofessional potential. Throughout this chapter and those that follow, we will draw from our own experiences with training and supervising paraprofessionals, including taking them from the point of employment to becoming members of a highly productive unit. We believe our model has something to offer any supervisor/trainer who works with nonprofessional employees, including those people working primarily with data and things rather than providing direct human service. Our point of view and greatest expertise, though, are directed toward human service. Few people are asked to do so much with so little and under such difficult circumstances as are human service paraprofessionals. How they are selected, trained, supported, and developed is critical to program success.

## OUR FRAME OF REFERENCE

We are approaching paraprofessional training from both developmental and competency-building perspectives. We view the human service paraprofessional as a learner who will experience growth along many domains. We believe that growth is a product of a well-designed initial training program, supported transition, ongoing training, and an effective performance management system.

Examples of growth dimensions include from dependent to independent; from rigid to flexible; from less mature to more mature; from concrete to abstract. In study after study of what today's workplace demands, employers report that they want their employees to exhibit initiative, flexibility, maturity, and problem-solving ability. Assuming that we want to see the same skills in our paraprofessionals, we have to provide a learning and growth environment. It is not that paraprofessionals lack these abilities—it is that they have generally lacked opportunities to develop them.

In addition to growth, our model emphasizes the development of competencies and the expected addition of new ones. The competencies should relate directly to performance management; that is, we must teach our paraprofessionals the competencies upon which we intend to evaluate their performance. These competencies should be reflected both in the job description and the performance appraisal instrument. After paraprofessionals are able to master the minimum competencies necessary to perform their jobs, they are free to develop additional ones as the needs and opportunities arise. A balance between growth and mastering tasks is necessary if we are to maximize paraprofessional potential.

We draw from the tenets of popular education where learners are treated as subjects instead of objects (Vella, 1994). In training practice, this stance represents the difference between lecturing trainees from a podium with occasional slides and overheads for those "visual people," and using strategies where participants actively engage in the learning process, practice new skills, and reflect upon what they have learned. We emphasize *dialogue* versus *monologue* throughout our model. People learn through exchanging ideas and through engaging in quality interactions with each other. Readers will be introduced to levels of interaction, with the lecture method representing the least interactive option.

We speak in terms of *designing*, that is, designing training, designing experiences, designing lessons, designing interview formats. We use *design* because it signifies being purposeful — and does not assume that growth and development and improved performance happen by some kind of osmosis. The beauty of our developmental and competency-building approach is twofold: (1) paraprofessionals become increasingly effective and self-reliant and (2) their supervisors are modeling what they want them to do with their clients. Of course, the ultimate reward is in program outcomes.

## WHAT IS REQUIRED OF SUPERVISORS

In this discussion about what is required of those who train and supervise paraprofessionals, we are going to assume that the training and supervisory function will be carried out by the same person, the supervisor. We recognize that not all readers have these direct responsibilities, but they may be responsible for those who do, or they may be considering what is involved when paraprofessionals are used to achieve desired human service outcomes.

1. *Supervisors will have to recognize the need to train the paraprofessionals and to build upon that training for as long as it takes for them to perform at or above expectations.* This statement may seem unnecessary because the need to train paraprofessionals is obvious. However, some organizations operate on

the assumption that once paraprofessionals have been exposed to content (such as nutrition, the basics of breastfeeding, the benefits of immunization, and so forth), their need for training diminishes. Olson (1994), in her review of paraprofessional training, found that the paraprofessionals continually asked for help in areas other than content, such as working with families in crisis, problem-solving strategies, teaching skills, managing difficult behavior, and managing multiple job components simultaneously. They knew from experience that knowledge of content was not enough to influence change. Much (if not all) of their training, however, was content based, stemming partly from the professionals' concern that any incorrect information reach the field. The following incident is an example of supervisors failing to understand the training role when they are responsible for human service paraprofessionals.

Six professionals were hired to administer a new program that was going to employ paraprofessionals to provide maternal and infant-health education to low-income women. These six people would be hiring and then training and supervising the paraprofessionals. They were aware of their job descriptions but had no idea what would be necessary to accomplish the goal of their program.

All six professionals attended a 4-day session designed to prepare them for their new positions. One of the first exercises required them to generate a list of what they thought their new paraprofessionals should be able to do and do well. Their trainer drew these items in the shape of a wheel, with the paraprofessional located at the center and the various competencies drawn as the spokes of the wheel. One by one, spokes were added as the supervisors offered their thoughts. "They need to be good record-keepers." Their trainer drew in a spoke representing good record keeping. "They have to be good listeners." SPOKE. "They have to plan their time well." SPOKE. "They have to know their subject backward and forward." SPOKE. "They have to be good persuaders and recruiters because people aren't required to participate in the program." SPOKE. As the number of spokes grew to 14, the trainer posed a new question to the group. "How do you think your paraprofessionals become good at all these skills?" At that moment—now marked by a stony silence—the supervisors' eyes widened. Then their questions began, one after another. "Don't we hire people who already have these skills?!" "Isn't someone else going to train them?" "Don't I have more important things to do?" Finally, the last questions were offered in an exasperated tone. "Do you mean we have to train them in all these areas? When?!"

Our research and experience indicate an organizational or supervisory resistance to providing comprehensive training and constant support and challenge to paraprofessionals. In some cases, the supervisors want to provide a more comprehensive training program but are not given that freedom by their own administrators. Some resistance to training may stem from different opinions on the role of the paraprofessional. Olson (1994) pointed out that some professionals believe that the paraprofessional will free them up to do more thoughtful and creative work.

Other professionals view the paraprofessional as having particular attributes and a wealth of previously untapped abilities that, with careful training and development, can be shaped and directed toward outstanding program outcomes. This second view embraces the idea that facilitating the growth and development of the paraprofessional is an important part of role of the supervising professional. Supervisors, of course, must commit to paraprofessional growth and development and recognize that a significant amount of time and planning need to be devoted toward attaining that goal.

2. *Supervisors must give as much attention to their teaching skills as they do to management or administrative skills.* Paraprofessionals are learners and their supervisors most often are their teachers. Perhaps supervisors have not thought of themselves in this way before. If programs are going to rely on paraprofessionals, then they must be taught the skills they need to perform successfully. The promise is made to new paraprofessionals that their life experiences are important and that they will be taught what they need to know about subject areas. "We will train you," programs advertise. To fulfill that promise, supervisors will want to develop their own teaching skills.

3. *Supervisors should become familiar with adult education principles and practices and apply them to their work settings.* They should familiarize themselves with adult learner motivation (Wlodowski, 1993), principles and practices of adult education (Knowles, 1980; Vella, 1994, 1995) and adult learning (Brookfield, 1986; Mezirow & Associates, 1990). As adult learners themselves, supervisors know a lot about learning, about what works well and what does not (at least for themselves). They must not assume, though, that what worked well for them will be appropriate for paraprofessionals. Exciting research is being done about multiple intelligences (Gardner, 1983; Lazear, 1994), revealing that many of the intelligences are virtually ignored in teaching and training. For example, the traditional lecture approach does not take advantage of learners' musical, kinesthetic, or visual spatial ways of knowing. Equally exciting are the revelations from the latest research on how the brain works and how it learns best (Caine & Caine, 1994; Rose & Nicholl, 1997). Supervisors need to acquire for themselves a thorough grounding in adult education and apply sound learning principles in their training activities.

4. *Supervisors must be willing to take risks, try new approaches, step out of their comfort zones, and learn.* It is easier to do things the way they have always been done. Change is difficult and heartily resisted, and taking risks requires courage. Paraprofessionals must be encouraged to take risks and not find their security in sticking to the old methods. Supervisors of paraprofessionals must resist the temptation to cling to practices which feel secure but which also hinder growth. After all, that is exactly what they are asking their human service paraprofessionals to do!

## DISTINCTIONS BETWEEN PROFESSIONALS AND PARAPROFESSIONALS

Both professionals and paraprofessionals bring with them to a work setting a wide range of personal characteristics and experiences. Some of what we define as characteristics will not be true of everyone. Nevertheless, our experience has led us to some observations that clearly distinguish paraprofessionals from professionals and thus indicate the need for a training approach that incorporates these differences. Knowledge of these differences gives administrators and supervisors a framework within which to make better hiring choices, provide appropriate initial training, offer supported transition, and manage performance.

## Characteristics and Distinctions

Paraprofessionals usually do not have college degrees. In many cases they possess, at most, a high school diploma. This important distinction has implications throughout one's involvement with paraprofessionals. The college graduate has a far greater experience with reading and writing, planning and prioritizing, being evaluated, studying content, handling abstractions, believing in one's own effectiveness, and thinking in terms of the future. We do not hold that paraprofessionals lack these abilities, but that they usually lack these experiences and the opportunity to develop more advanced skills.

When we hire professionals, we are in a sense "buying" their content-oriented knowledge base and expertise in areas such as nutrition, child development, maternal health, social work, geriatrics, and immunization. With paraprofessionals, however, we are "buying" their life experiences, and we will have to teach them the appropriate content.

Professionals usually have had considerable work experience in more formal work settings. Even if they are quite young, they have had related experiences through college internships, leadership roles, and work-study assignments. Many paraprofessionals, on the other hand, are taking their very first job in a formal work setting.

Professionals recognize some sense of their value to the organization, vis-à-vis their salary and benefit status. Paraprofessionals, in many cases, have never been paid for their work or were paid only for work done on the spot and not within a salary format.

Professionals are accustomed to continuously learning content and concepts in order to keep pace with the new knowledge that is revealed by research and technology. They have developed helpful strategies to that end. Paraprofessionals, in most cases, have not been in situations that required them to keep pace with an ever-changing body of knowledge and will lack the kinds of learning strategies that professionals take for granted.

Professionals usually have already proved to themselves that they are successful learners. Paraprofessionals, by contrast, may be coming to their positions with very poor experiences in education and a resulting lack of confidence in themselves.

Professionals are generally accustomed to either supervising or being supervised and handling feedback, both positive and negative. Paraprofessionals are, by and large, not accustomed to being supervised and constantly evaluated.

Managing multiple work tasks simultaneously and within preestablished time frames, while difficult for most people, is expected of professionals. For many of them, this requirement is part of the appeal of the job. Paraprofessionals will probably be new at such task management within time limitations.

Professionals generally have a respectable tolerance for ambiguity, for the world "between the lines," for the nuances and twists and lack of straight lines. Paraprofessionals will often be quite frustrated with ambiguity or will not recognize it.

Paraprofessionals bring with them a wealth of life experiences that allow them to form relationships with clients, to empathize (but not sympathize) with them, and as a result, to affect behavior change. They are often role models for the clients they serve, an embodiment of what is possible. They may not have college experience, a resume, or comfort with abstractions. They may never have been on a salary. What they do have, however, is a desire to make a difference and the courage to accept a human service paraprofessional position in the first place. The supervisor's responsibility is to plan for their development, while at the same time improving program outcomes. Supervisors must avoid the assumption that paraprofessionals will train themselves or that they will pick it up from someone else. Supervisors certainly cannot assume that paraprofessionals will learn the way their supervisors did and benefit from the same training methods.

## THE SEQUENTIAL DEVELOPMENT MODEL FOR MAXIMIZING PARAPROFESSIONAL POTENTIAL

Facing a new group of human service paraprofessionals— many of whom have never worked before and most of whom are quite anxious about their own abilities and this organization— can be a humiliating experience. It can also be trial-and-error if the supervisor has not trained paraprofessionals in the past or simply has not had the time that is required to develop people. The Sequential Development Model offers a solution—a framework—that can guide supervisors (and all others involved) through all phases of paraprofessional development (see Figure 1.1). The model comprises six major areas, and a chapter is devoted to each area, complete with specific examples. The six areas are job task analysis; selection and hiring; initial training; supported transition; ongoing training; and performance management.

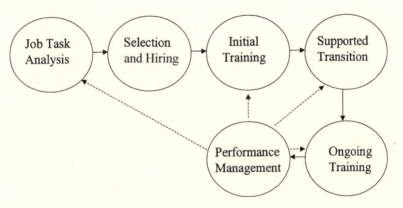

**Figure 1.1** The Sequential Development Model for Maximizing Paraprofessional Potential

## Job Task Analysis

What will the paraprofessionals be asked to do, to know, and to be? Doing such an analysis for paraprofessional positions is important for at least three reasons:

1. Supervisors must be clear about what they are hiring paraprofessionals to do so that they will know what evidence of skills to look for during the selection process. They must be equally clear about what paraprofessionals are not being asked to do;

2. Supervisors need to clarify how much content knowledge their paraprofessionals will actually need to master. It may not be as much as originally thought or it may be more. Supervisors may learn that they are interested in skills that are far more important than the possession of content knowledge; and:

3. By doing a thorough job task analysis, supervisors can begin to quantify the kind of time, planning and commitment that will be required for the training enterprise.

Chapter 2 describes the Job Task Analysis process. The first step is to determine the basic work skills supervisors wish to see in their paraprofessionals before any formal training takes place. The second step is to analyze the particular job and determine what specific skills and attributes are required at the time of hiring. Finally, indicators for those skills and attributes have to be chosen. How does the supervisor know a particular employee possesses a work-related skill?

## Selection and Hiring

Few decisions are as important for ensuring the success of any human service program than who is hired to provide the services. We believe this especially applies to human service paraprofessionals. Chapter 3 contains a description of the three major components for selection and hiring paraprofessionals: (1) setting up the hiring process; (2) preparing for the interview process; and (3) choosing successful candidates.

Setting up the hiring process for paraprofessionals calls for specific strategies and practices, which may be in many ways quite different from those utilized when hiring professionals. The interviewing must be designed specifically for paraprofessionals. Final decisions should be based on a variety of indicators specific to what the paraprofessionals will be asked to do.

## Initial Training

The initial training component, discussed in Chapter 4, involves making four decisions that address these important questions:

1. What should be included in the training?

2. Who will conduct the training?

3. How should the training be designed?

4. How should the training be evaluated?

The initial training that paraprofessionals receive sets the tone for their future accomplishments. We place a great deal of emphasis on the development of respect and safety in the learning and work environment, which continues to pay dividends throughout our model. When executed properly, initial training will result in employees who are considerably more skilled than when they were hired and who confidently take risks and ask questions.

## Supported Transition

To ensure continued learning and development, new paraprofessionals need a period of supported transition. During this time, individual relationships with paraprofessionals are strengthened. Supervisors encourage them to voice their questions and concerns. Also, supervisors model behaviors they want the paraprofessionals to emulate (such as problem solving, teaching, questioning). Supervisors continue to build respect and safety, develop skills, and lay the groundwork for a well-functioning team. Chapter 5 includes a discussion of the need for supported transition and strategies to implement it.

## Ongoing Training

When minimum competencies are mastered, that is, when paraprofessionals can do their jobs and feel good about it, ongoing training is possible. The need for ongoing training manifests itself in several ways, each of which supervisors should recognize. Supervisors will also choose training venues and formats that are appropriate for paraprofessional training. Finally, supervisors (and anyone else providing training) are charged with designing training procedures that are most effective with paraprofessionals. Chapters 4 and 6 include sample training designs that readers may use for models.

## Performance Management

The topic of performance appraisal is often accompanied by negative thoughts and attitudes. Chapter 7 presents performance appraisal as an integral component of a comprehensive performance management system. The multiple components of this larger system are identified, and a step-by-step approach to an effective performance appraisal is included.

## Using the Sequential Development Model

The Sequential Development Model was created to meet the unique staff development needs of paraprofessionals. The six components are steps that should be addressed initially in the order of job task analysis, selection and hiring, initial training, supported transition, ongoing training, and performance management. The Model also represents a *process* which is denoted by the solid lines on Figure 1.1. The results of performance management will determine the next step. For example, if performance is exemplary, ongoing training would be the next step. If however, performance is below average, supervisors may need to conduct remedial training (the initial training component) or provide more individual coaching (supported transition). These steps are denoted by dotted lines on the model diagram.

## SUMMARY

We have set the stage for maximizing paraprofessional potential. By now readers should have a clearer sense of what is being asked of them. We recognize that readers will be coming to this discussion with different responsibilities, including an overview responsibility for all the professional staff who will then be responsible for the paraprofessionals. We offer our model especially to those who have direct responsibility for the paraprofessionals, knowing that others will select the material they find valuable. Although our model is developed as an entire process, parts of it may be selected for immediate use. Chapter 8 concludes this volume with a brief discussion of issues and concerns related to using paraprofessionals, and with a review of small but powerful strategies supervisors can employ to obtain immediate program results.

# CHAPTER 2

## Job Task Analysis

In order to succeed in their work, what will paraprofessional need to *do*? What must they *know*? What must they *be* in order to do their jobs well? To make the link among job description, interview, training, and performance management, it is necessary to determine what these employees will be asked to do. That determination comes from analyzing the actual position. Fortunately, much information about basic job skills is already available in a generic form and can be applied to a specific job.

## THE RESEARCH

O'Neil, Allred, and Baker (1992) reviewed five studies of workforce readiness to determine the studies' similarities and differences. These studies included

(1) What Work Requires of Schools (U.S. Dept. of Labor, June, 1991), which is usually referred to as the SCANS report;

(2) Workplace Basics: The Essential Skills Employers Want, conducted by the American Society for Training and Development (ASTD) with the support of the U.S. Department of Labor (Carnevale, Gainer, & Metzler, 1990a);

(3) High Schools and the Changing Workplace: The Employers' View, developed by the National Academy of Sciences; (1984), and

(4) Studies conducted in Michigan (Mehrens, 1989) and New York (New York State Department of Education, 1990),

both attempting to establish the basic skills employees need on the job.

## The Research Findings

O'Neil et al. (1992) found that four categories of skills and characteristics appeared in four of the five studies they reviewed. Each study revealed the need for basic academic skills, such as reading, writing, arithmetic, listening, and speaking. Second, all five of the studies identified the need for higher order thinking skills. O'Neil et al. observed that the most common higher order thinking skills identified can be seen as skills in adapting to the rapid changes in the workforce. In four of the studies, problem-solving skills were included in higher order thinking skills, with employees able to think creatively, make decisions, separate fact from opinion, and reason. One study included working out new ways of handling recurring problems and "determining what is needed to accomplish a work assignment" as higher order thinking skills. Interestingly, some of these higher-order thinking skills might be more easily seen as the objectives of paraprofessionals' training after the initial selection process has been completed.

The third category of skills that all the studies had in common was referred to as interpersonal and teamwork skills. These skills were regarded as the most important, even though they were also the most diversely described and the most difficult to fine-tune into subsets. The SCANS report referred to interpersonal competencies while the ASTD report spoke of group effectiveness skills. The National Academy of Science wrote about interpersonal relationship skills. Although difficult to define and broadly interpreted, it is clear that getting along with others was deemed as a critical workplace skill according to the workplace reports. We believe that a deeper examination of these interpersonal and teamwork skills will bear considerable fruit when hiring and then training paraprofessionals. After all, we are usually looking for a certain set of interpersonal skills that allow our paraprofessionals to establish relationships with clients. It is worth the effort to more clearly name what we mean.

The fourth category common to all these studies was not a set of skills but rather personal characteristics and attitudes. For example, the SCANS report referred to Personal Qualities-Foundation, which included responsibility, self-esteem, sociability, integrity, honesty and self-management. The Michigan study included "communicating with all members of the group, using a team approach to solve problems, and showing sensitivity to the thoughts and opinions of others in a group" (Mehrens, 1989, p. 9). The Michigan results also indicated that demonstrating self-esteem, motivation, and responsibility were often rated by employers as being more critical than the other workforce skills.

## Applying the Research to Paraprofessional Positions

How can these findings be used to help in the hiring and training of paraprofessionals? First, the results of these studies may be placed in the context of the paraprofessional setting. For instance, some of the skills seen as prerequisites for entering the job may instead be goals for paraprofessional training after employment has begun. Second, certain skills may not be covered in these studies. For example, the ability to juggle multiple tasks simultaneously did not appear in the reviewed studies and yet is crucial to paraprofessional success in many situations. Also not addressed was something as simple as the ability to read a city or county street map, an absolute must-have skill for paraprofessional outreach workers. By comparing the findings of the workplace studies with program requirements, a basic set of entry-level work skills may be established.

## Seven Categories for Paraprofessional Job Task Analysis

For our job task analysis model, we use the four major skills and attributes areas found in all the studies: basic academic; higher order thinking; interpersonal and teamwork; and personal characteristics and attitudes. Because we are focusing on human services, we break basic academic skills into two categories: basic academic and communication skills. Even though speaking and listening skills are commonly included in definitions of literacy and basic academic skills, we believe they should be addressed separately. Potential paraprofessionals may have completed a high school or GED program, for instance, but this completion does not ensure that their speaking and listening skills have been developed.

The sixth category for job task analysis is previous knowledge, which allows us to ascertain what specific knowledge paraprofessionals should bring with them to the job. *Knowledge* in this case may be more related to experience (for example, having breastfed a child) than to any kind of subject matter. Finally, we add a seventh category to cover technical skills. It is possible a paraprofessional will need to have certain technical expertise (such as understanding the basics of using a computer) at the outset rather than after further training.

## SETTING UP THE JOB TASK ANALYSIS

Carnevale et al. (1990b) offer a straightforward job task analysis plan that distinguishes among a job, a duty, a task, and a step. A job is a "specific position requiring the performance of specific tasks" (p. 4). A duty is an "arbitrary clustering of related tasks into broad functional areas of responsibility" (p. 4). A task is a "work activity that is discrete, observable, performed within a limited time period and leads to a product, service, or decision" (p. 4). A task is made up of two or more steps. A job task analysis consists of listing each duty, then identifying the tasks and steps that comprise the duty. Although a more detailed analysis is possible, we are carrying such an analysis only as far as is practical.

### Analyzing a New Position

What happens if the program or position is brand new and no experience exists upon which to conduct a job task analysis? For example, a state organization may have just received funding for an outreach program that will employ paraprofessionals to serve senior adults. Supervisors will need to look elsewhere for an analysis. One possibility is to use the three-pronged assessment model proposed by Vella (1995), which is to ask, study, and observe. Supervisors can contact administrators of similar programs, preferably in related areas and circumstances. They can interview key staff and ask, "What skills have your people needed? Which ones are the most important? Which skills were you looking for in the interview process and which skills did you subsequently teach?" Documents can be reviewed about other programs, both similar and related. Finally, supervisors can arrange to observe a similar program in action and spend at least a day with the paraprofessionals, in order to ask them the same questions.

## Analyzing an Existing Position

If a program is already in operation, a job task analysis can certainly be done more accurately. Supervisors may conduct the analysis themselves by reviewing documents that address job descriptions, position announcements and performance appraisals. A key question of the existing program would be, "Is the current system successful at changing behaviors?" It is also important to validate findings with the existing paraprofessionals. Do they agree with the lists of tasks and skills? What would they delete? Add? Emphasize? What have they been asked to do?

## PARAPROFESSIONAL JOB TASK ANALYSES

We offer three examples of the results of job task analyses for three different paraprofessional positions. For each position, we use categories of basic academic skills, higher order thinking skills, interpersonal skills, communication skills, personal attributes, experience knowledge, and technical skills. The first example, Figure 2.1, is an extension program assistant position.

Administrators and/or supervisors determine which skills must be identified on the application or during the interview

JOB:      Extension Nutrition Program Assistant (a paraprofessional employed by the Cooperative Extension service of any given state)

DUTY:     To provide nutrition education to groups of limited-resource families.

TASKS:    1. Recruit at least six new families per month into the program.
          2. Provide nutrition lessons to three groups per week.
          3. Collect and record all necessary data.

SKILLS:   (the skills required to accomplish the tasks)

Basic Academic Skills:
- Read
- Write
- Measure
- Count
- Recall
- Memorize

Higher Order Thinking Skills:
- Know how to learn
- Know how to prioritize
- Know how to design equivalents
- Know how to create and manage materials
- Know how to clarify
- Know how to manage multiple tasks

Interpersonal/Teamwork Skills:
- Plan with a co-teacher
- Co-teach
- Network
- Empathize
- Assess feelings

Communication Skills:
- Explain
- Ask
- Teach
- Demonstrate
- Persuade
- Inform
- Use a telephone to call clients
- Listen
- Paraphrase
- Echo
- Clarify
- Interview

Personal Attributes:
- Flexible
- Organized
- Genuine
- Caring
- Motivated
- Punctual

**Figure 2.1.** Job task analysis of extension nutrition program assistant.

Personal Attributes: (continued)
- Respectful
- Affirming
- Safe
- Sincere
- Friendly

- Self-respecting
- Calm
- Mature
- Able to relate

Experience in/or Knowledge of:
- Living on a limited budget
- Shopping for bargains

- Basic food safety
- Feeding a family

Technical Skills:
- Operating kitchen equipment
- Cooking
- Baking

**Figure 2.1.** Job task analysis of extension nutrition program assistant. (continued)

and which skills may be taught in training. For example, managing multiple tasks, a very important skill for the nutrition program assistant, may be taught in both informal and formal training. We caution supervisors not to make the mistake of overlooking or ruling out potentially excellent paraprofessionals because they may not have all the skills necessary for some tasks. Also, some skills may be—and some should be—taught over time. In hiring human service paraprofessionals, the life experiences (in this case living on a limited budget) may take precedence over other skills. We emphasize that the purpose of the job task analysis is to help supervisors ascertain what skills paraprofessionals should bring with them to the job. The analysis will also illuminate additional areas of training that may be needed. Supervisors, therefore, will be looking for evidence that the applicant can learn new skills.

Our second job task analysis example (Figure 2.2) is for a telephone hotline worker position.

In every instance of job task analysis, supervisors have to be realistic about the time and resources for training that are available to them. In the case of the hotline worker, it may be more important to hire paraprofessionals who already have ex-

JOB:        Hotline Worker for a state-operated Medicaid/Managed-Care program

DUTY:       To respond to all incoming calls to the Hotline.

TASKS:      1. Operate a multiline telephone system.
            2. Retrieve information from the appropriate computerized databases.
            3. Provide the caller with the requested information, or refer the caller to the proper respondent.

SKILLS:     (the skills required to accomplish the tasks)

Basic Academic Skills:
- Read
- Write
- Spell
- Record
- Scan
- Memorize
- Sort

Higher Order Thinking Skills:
- Compare
- Contrast
- Attention to detail
- Time management
- Decision making
- Problem solving

Interpersonal/Teamwork Skills:
- Respect other staff members
- Recognize emotions
- Plan in cooperation with others
- Show empathy
- Accept evaluation

Communication Skills:
- Speak clearly
- Listen
- Explain
- Announce intentions
- Clarify
- Paraphrase
- Resolve conflict

Personal Attributes:
- Friendly
- Pleasant voice
- Calm
- Stamina

Experience in/or Knowledge of:
- Using computers
- Working with the public

Technical Skills:
- Operating a multiline telephone system

**Figure 2.2.** Job task analysis for telephone hotline worker.

JOB:      Breastfeeding Counselor
DUTY:     To help new mothers overcome common barriers associ-
          ated with breastfeeding their infants.
TASKS:    1. Establish personal contact with all eligible new mothers
          while they are still in the hospital.
          2. Make at least one home-teaching visit to these enrolled
          mothers; make repeat visits as necessary.
          3. Collect and record all relevant data for the program.
SKILLS:   (the skills required to accomplish the tasks)

Basic Academic Skills:
- Read                        - Count
- Write                       - Record
- Memorize                    - Recall

Higher Order Thinking Skills:
- Manage multiple tasks       - Map reading
- Attention to detail         - Problem solving
- Decision making

Interpersonal/Teamwork Skills:
- Understand ("read") the situation
- Empathize
- Relate

Communication Skills:
- Speak clearly               - Clarify
- Explain well                - Paraphrase
- Listen                      - Echo
- Ask open-ended questions
- Show appropriate body-language

Personal Attributes:
- Friendly                    - Good in a crisis
- Calm                        - Soothing

Experience in/or Knowledge of:
- Breastfeeding (personal experience)

Technical Skills:
- Operating a digital pager
- Operating a computer

**Figure 2.3.** Job task analysis for breastfeeding counselor.

tensive telephone experience than to assume that adequate time and personnel will be available to train them.

Our third example is a breastfeeding counselor position (Figure 2.3)

Candidates chosen for these positions probably will be taught the necessary technical skills after they are hired. However, by analyzing the job in advance, supervisors and other interviewers can design interview questions that determine if candidates have prerequisite skills and provide evidence of their ability to learn new skills.

## ADDITIONAL CONSIDERATIONS WHILE ANALYZING TASKS

### Clarifying What We Really Want

It is very easy to look for too many entry qualifications! Upon further analysis, certain skills, knowledge, experiences, and attributes may not be necessary in order to successfully perform a job. For example, let us consider the skill of *writing*. For what purposes will the paraprofessionals use their writing skills? Will they be communicating with clients or other agency personnel in writing? Will writing be used primarily for recording basic data? The writing issue can come up quite strongly when selecting paraprofessionals whose first language is not English. Exactly what will the paraprofessionals be required to write? They may very quickly learn to record the necessary data for official forms or ask other paraprofessionals to help them. A similar skills category is *speaking*. In what language (or languages) will business be conducted? Is it necessary for paraprofessionals to be able to speak more than one language? Or does the term "speaking skills" refer chiefly to one's ability to articulate clearly? Does it have more to do with presentation skills?

What is meant by saying we want to hire people who *relate* to their clientele? Can relating be broken down into skills that may be taught and acquired? Must a paraprofessional have a similar background, experience and socioeconomic status to the clients in order to be an effective teacher or counselor? What additional factors might be equally or even more important?

The national studies on workforce preparedness indicate the importance of possessing *interpersonal* skills. What are these skills and what do they mean in each work setting? Goleman (1995) refers to emotional intelligence, which includes such interpersonal skills as the ability to read the room; to understand what is happening emotionally; and to empathize with and soothe others. Can these skills be more finely defined and then taught? Do administrators and supervisors rely too much on instinct about who should be hired, thus placing too little emphasis on clearly defining highly valued interpersonal skills? A common supervisory refrain is, "But she interviewed so well!" The more clarity supervisors have about what they want in a human service paraprofessional, the more likely that they can construct an interview format which will reveal those skills and attributes.

## Avoiding Overreliance on Discrete-Skill Identification

Finally, some researchers in adult education take issue with what they consider to be a misguided attempt to reduce human skills into small, discrete components. According to Mezirow and Associates (1990), this reductionist strategy completely discounts the context within which people learn, work, and communicate. It ignores the sum of their parts and the complexities of being human. Any analysis of tasks must be tempered with an appreciation for human potential. Also, it would be impossible to remove the subjective component from interview decisions. What is possible is to better clarify which skills paraprofessionals need to bring with them to the job.

We offer these thoughts in addition to examples of job task analyses so that those who are responsible for hiring and training paraprofessionals may further refine their own thinking and create models that reflect their own situations. At this point, we are ready to move to the next component in our six-step plan to maximize paraprofessional potential: selection and hiring.

# CHAPTER 3

## Selection and Hiring

Selecting and hiring the right people for certain positions is often the most difficult and yet most critical facet of supervision (Galbraith, Sisco, & Guglielmino, 1997). Specialists in the area of communications tell us that the impression we make during the first 90 seconds of contact with other people very much determines our fate with them (Peoples, 1992; Wilder, 1994). [Supervisors should ask themselves if hiring decisions about paraprofessionals are being made in just 90 seconds.] Perhaps some supervisors have been served well by the affective components of an interview, going on feelings and instincts that a certain professional is right for the job. Of course, these supervisors also had other indicators to guide them from the beginning. They were looking for a particular professional degree and type of work experience that applied to the needs of their programs. When adding these indicators to letters of recommendation and other references, they may have felt confident to base their final decisions on more affective factors.

What are the indicators for screening applicants for paraprofessional positions? Supervisors may be asking only for a high school credential. The experience they would like to see may not come from traditional employment, but instead from life circumstances. Many candidates will lack extensive work histories. As noted earlier, it is common to have applicants with no work history at all, particularly among female applicants. At the same time, it is not unusual to have scores of applicants for a position in certain geographical areas, particularly if the position offers benefits such as health insurance. How can the right people be selected when those doing the selecting must rely on nontraditional indicators? In this chapter we examine some proven strategies for selecting and hiring paraprofessionals. The entire process is addressed, from describing and announcing the position, to making the offer.

## THE PRELIMINARY STEPS

### Setting Aside the Time

Time is a critical factor we wish to emphasize at the outset in the selecting, hiring, and training processes for paraprofessionals. Supervisors are busy people with numerous responsibilities and demands on their time. Yet to maximize opportunities for success with paraprofessionals, sufficient time must be available. In addition, supervisors are responsible for coordinating schedules of other key figures involved in selecting and hiring to assure that they will be available when needed. Once the interviewing has begun, schedules should be cleared sufficiently to accomplish the interviews without large gaps in time. And, most important, supervisors must continue to be available throughout the training. They should not assume that paraprofessionals will be equipped to deal with ambiguities in scheduling, changes in plans, shifts in priorities and unexpected waiting. It has been our experience that selecting and hiring paraprofessionals requires more structure than hiring professionals.

### Developing the Job Description

Before actually writing a job description for the paraprofessional position, supervisors should consult their organization's policies. Do guidelines exist for writing job descriptions? Does the organization currently hire paraprofessionals? If the answer is "no," it may be necessary to explain to administrators both the purpose and the advantages of hiring paraprofessionals. In addition, supervisors will need to have a clear understanding of employee benefits available to paraprofessionals as well as how many hours per week they must work in order to qualify for them. Supervisors should not underestimate the importance of benefits to their applicants, particularly if health insurance is one of them. The retention rate of paraprofessionals is often more directly related to employee benefits than salary.

We now turn our attention to the job description. The principal elements should include the job title, the basic duties of the job, some examples of specific job tasks, and the status of the position (for instance, temporary or permanent, part-time or full-time). The job description may need to be quite detailed. An example:

JOB TITLE:   Extension Nutrition Teaching Assistant,
             permanent part-time, 30 hours per week.

DUTY:        Teach nutrition to individuals and groups
             of low-income families.

TASKS:       Recruit 7–10 new families per month;
             Teach 3–6 groups per week;
             Collect and record all necessary data;
             Graduate 7–10 families per month.

Final approval for the job description may be required from the organization's human resources department. At the same time, they may be consulted about placing a job advertisement.

## Writing the Job Advertisement

We recommend that the job advertisement answer these questions:

1. What is the title of the position?

2. When will it be available?

3. What does it pay?

4. What kind of work is it?

5. How does one get an application?

6. When is the application deadline?

7. What are the educational requirements?

8. What, if any, work experience is required?

9. How many hours per week will the employee work?

Our example, Figure 3.1, shows an advertisement for a Breast-feeding Counselor position.

## Considerations for Placing the Advertisement and Handling the Results

When the advertisement is complete, a timeline should be established for the advertisement period, interview process, start date, initial training, supported transition period, and probationary review date (if applicable). Again, it is important to remember that with paraprofessionals, structure and continuity are very important.

What factors should be considered when advertising a human service paraprofessional position? We pose seven questions (or areas) for consideration:

1. Who is the target audience? Who is most likely to be interested in this type of position? Where would they look for employment possibilities?

2. In what publications will advertisements be placed? If the paraprofessional will concentrate time in one region of the county, for example, then the advertisement should appear in a smaller, regional newspaper as well as a major municipal publication.

3. Where should advertisements be placed? If the paraprofessional will promote immunization of infants and toddlers, notices may be posted on bulletin boards in the waiting rooms of health departments, in child health clinics, and in physicians'

Position Title:      Breastfeeding Counselor
Location:            Weston County, N.C.
Available:           July 1, 1997
Responsibilities:    Provide in-home support for breastfeeding mothers
                     who give birth at Weston County Medical Center.
Hours Per Week:      30
Salary:              $14,000 annual
Benefits:            Health, retirement, vacation leave, sick leave
Qualifications:      A high school diploma (or equivalent). Preference
                     will be given to persons with personal breastfeed-
                     ing experience. A valid driver's license and the use
                     of a personal automobile.
Apply To:            Cooperative Extension/Weston County Center
                     401 Grand Highway, Bldg. B
                     Westontown, NC 12345

Applications may be obtained from: Cooperative Extension Service, Weston County Center, Westontown, N.C., Monday–Friday, 8am–5pm. Applications will be accepted until 5:00 p.m., June 1, 199__. If they are mailed to us, they must be received in our office by 5:00 p.m., June 1, 199__. They may be hand-delivered by 5:00 p.m., June 1, 199__, Attention: Sarah Sutton.

For additional information, contact Jane McBride, Program Coordinator.

*North Carolina Cooperative Extension Service is an Equal Opportunity Employer and seeks to employ the best qualified individual without regard to race, color, religion, age, sex or national origin.*

**Figure 3.1.** A position announcement for a paraprofessional breastfeeding counselor.

offices. In other words, openings should be publicized where potential clients are likely to see them. After all, potential clients may also be potential paraprofessionals.

    4. Will applicant screening be conducted by an employment service or the organization's human resources department? It is probably best for the supervisor to screen the applicants. It is often difficult for supervisors (especially first-time supervisors)

to describe to an employment service or to the human services department exactly what attributes they seek in an applicant, because this is a matter of great subjectivity. An employment service may eliminate too many applicants from the pool, or it may eliminate none. In either case, precious time is lost without having gained much assistance.

5. What process is preferred for receiving applications? Telephone numbers should appear in the advertisement only if telephone inquiries from potential applicants are desired. If the business name and address are given, some applicants will find the phone number and call. So, if telephone inquiries are definitely not wanted, a brief statement to that effect should appear in the advertisement, such as "No phone calls, please." The organization may prefer to receive letters of inquiry by way of a blind-box address at a newspaper or employment agency, although this method is not particularly applicant-friendly. (A street address to which completed applications may be mailed or hand-delivered is certainly more inviting.) Deadlines for receiving applications should be clearly indicated.

Applicants for paraprofessional positions may hesitate to apply because of a lack of confidence in their abilities, and they may wait until the deadline date to hand-deliver their applications. Many applicants will call to ask for clarification of the requirements. Such calls often result in completed applications and ultimately exemplary employees. For this reason, including a phone number in an advertisement may be advisable. If telephone inquiries will be accepted, individuals answering the telephone should be informed about the advertisement and know where to direct calls.

6. For what length of time should the advertisement run? The length of time an advertisement needs to run depends on the rate of unemployment in the area as well as the number of paraprofessionals to be hired. In an urban area, a notice published in a major newspaper may result in 60–80 applications. In a rural area, by contrast, the number of responses may be far lower.

7. Will copies of the job application be available? The or-

ganization's standard application should be reviewed carefully for sections that may not be applicable to paraprofessionals. After modification, copies should be available for potential applicants and placed in a convenient location. Also, as with the telephone inquiries mentioned earlier, someone in the office should know about the applications, where they are located, and who may be asking for them.

## Reviewing the Applications

After the closing date has passed, each application should be thoroughly reviewed. If some applications are to be eliminated at this point, the criteria for making such decisions should be established. For example, an application may be eliminated if the applicant clearly does not have the desired experience, does not have the minimum education required, or does not reside in the appropriate county. Applicants who are not going to be considered, for whatever reasons, should be notified of that decision and given the basis for it. A file should be created for each of the remaining applicants.

The next step is to mail out requests for references. We recommend this step be implemented now because it often takes a considerable amount of time for references to come back. Previous employers appreciate a checklist rather than an open-ended request for reference. The human resources staff may already have such a checklist. Before developing or modifying a form, they should be consulted.

## PREPARING FOR THE INTERVIEW PROCESS

## The Group Information Session

If only a few applicants are involved, individual interviews may start immediately. However, if the applicant group is large in relation to the number of openings, we recommend a different strategy, one particularly applicable to hiring paraprofessionals: offering a group-information session for the applicants. A group information session provides an opportunity both for the applicants and the supervisor to learn more about each other. Some applicants may not be clear about what the job entails. Other applicants may be facing their first real opportunity to hold a salaried position and will have many questions and uncertainties about what is expected of them. After hearing more about the position and asking questions, some applicants may choose to withdraw their applications.

The group information session allows supervisors to associate names with faces and to observe the applicants interacting with people they do not know. The group information session partially compensates for the lack of the usual hiring indicators (such as level of education, type of degree, and related experience).

Cards should be mailed to the applicants inviting them to the information sessions with an explanation that other applicants may also be present. The card should detail what the applicants may expect to learn at the session. Applicants should be asked to bring their appointment calendars with them. The supervisor's calendar should be cleared for interviews, as interested applicants will be invited to schedule their individual interviews before leaving.

Figure 3.2 is an example of an invitation to a group information session. Administrators and/or supervisors will determine if all applicants will receive the invitation or if the applicant pool will be screened before the group information session. Also, if attendance at the group session is required in order to be considered for a position, applicants should be so advised. An additional decision to consider may be the number of group sessions to hold, particularly if the applicant group is very large. Supervisors may offer both a day and an evening group information session for the applicants' convenience.

What should be included in a group information session? Based on our own experiences, we offer a format that has been

---

**Marsha Jones**
**580 Titusville Rd., Apt. 3N**
**Westontown, N.C. 12349**

Congratulations! <u>Your application for employment</u> for the para-professional position of Nutrition Education Program Assistant <u>is currently under review</u>. You are invited to attend a group information session designed for you and other applicants, on **Monday March 10, 1997, at 9:00 A.M., OR on Tuesday March 11, at 3:00 P.M.,** in Room 22-A of the Cooperative Extension Service/Weston County Center, 401 Grand Highway, Bldg. B., in Westontown. The session should last about 1-to 1–1/2 hours. **<u>In order for your application to be further considered, you must attend one of these sessions</u>**. Other applicants (whose applications are also under review) will attend the information session. We will provide information about the position—its responsibilities; the organization—its structure and programs; some of the benefits offered with this position, etc. We will answer any questions you may have about the position and the organization. And we will provide a calendar for you to schedule an individual interview for a later date. Light refreshments will be available following the session. *Please bring your appointment calendar with you!*

Kindly call this office by 3:00 p.m. on Thursday, March 6th, to reserve a seat *at the information session of your choice.* Our number is 555–9999—ask for Sarah Sutton. We look forward to seeing you at one of the sessions!

---

**Figure 3.2**. Example of an invitation to a group information session.

quite successful. Figure 3.3 outlines a typical group information session.

The goal of the group information session is to explain the program purpose, objectives, delivery methods, job expectations, personnel policies, and employment benefits.

The room should be arranged to help applicants be as comfortable as possible, avoiding a classroom-type atmosphere. For

1. Before the session
   - Prepare nametags for everyone attending the session;
   - Develop a schedule for individual interviews;
   - Arrange the room; prepare refreshments.
2. Welcome. Thank the applicants for their interest in the position(s).
3. Give a brief introduction/history of the organization.
4. Introduce the specific program.
5. Explain the paraprofessional position(s) available.
6. Review the job responsibilities, expectations, and basic eligibility requirements.
7. Explain employment procedures, hours, pay, benefits, and training.
8. Discuss specific information, including the following:
   - The need for reliable transportation;
   - The type of work the paraprofessional(s) will do;
   - Any physical requirements of the job;
   - Performance evaluation procedures;
   - Any other particulars about the job.
9. Questions-and-Answers.
10. Thank applicants once more for attending the group session.
11. Provide a schedule for applicants to sign up for individual interviews; ask them to sign up now if they are still interested in the position(s).

**Figure 3.3**. Format for conducting a group information session.

instance, chairs may be placed in a semicircle or circle. Simple, light refreshments will help to put applicants at ease. Handout materials may be provided. The time immediately following the session may be used for informal interactions with applicants and for giving them an opportunity to sign up for interviews.

Individual interview appointments should be transferred to the supervisor's calendar and the applicant files should be placed in the order of the interview schedule. Letters of reference should be added to each file as they are received. Finally, the interviews may begin. We provide a sample interview checklist (Figure 3.4) that should help supervisors organize the total process.

## PREPARATION CHECKLIST FOR THE INTERVIEW PROCESS

___ Determine a time frame for the total process.

___ Coordinate calendars of all those who need to be involved in the interview.

___ Check the organization's policies for job descriptions.

___ Get a clear understanding of paraprofessional policies and benefits.

___ Develop the job description.

___ Consult with human resources regarding approval of the job description and advertising.

___ Write the job advertisement.

___ Establish a detailed time line for the entire process, including the advertisement, interviews, start dates, training dates.

___ Place the ad with the newspaper or other publication.

___ Do an initial screening of applicants, if desired.

___ Schedule the group information session(s).

___ Invite applicants to the group session.

___ Plan the group session, including handout materials, location, refreshments, etc.

___ Schedule interviews, either from the group session or individually (if there is no group session planned).

___ Place applicant files in the order in which interviews will be conducted.

**Figure 3.4**. Preparation checklist for the interview process.


# THE INTERVIEW PROCESS


## Preparing for Successful Interviews

Where does one begin when this is the first experience with interviewing for paraprofessional positions or if the process has been less than successful in the past? The first contact should be with the human resources department for clarification of interview guidelines and procedures. Do standard questions exist for all applicants? Should additional questions be the same for all applicants? Must the questions first be approved? Organizational policies should be clarified right away.

It is not difficult to find information about interviewing. It is difficult to find information that relates specifically to interviewing paraprofessionals. Beatty (1995) lists six areas that typically interest interviewers: technical competence, job motivation, fit with work environment, fit with boss, interpersonal relationships, and areas for improvement. Of the 46 questions to which he suggests employers seek answers, 26 relate specifically to an applicant's work history. However, applicants for paraprofessional positions may not have any work history or certainly not enough history to help the interviewing supervisor detect patterns and trends.

Supervisors are basically looking for people who can do the job, who are motivated to do the job, and who will fit into the work environment. We recommend three strategies that should help supervisors determine this fit: use job task analysis; consider other indicators for proof of the desired skills or attributes; and arrange the interview room to make the applicant feel safe.

1. Use the job task analysis. In Chapter 2, we described seven categories of skills or attributes: basic academic skills, higher order thinking skills, interpersonal/relationship skills, communications skills, experience/knowledge, personal attributes, and technical skills. Interview questions may be developed that target each of these areas or those most important to the position. If, for example, candidates are being interviewed for a maternal health outreach position (a job that will require considerable listening and mentoring skills), questions should be formulated to address those particular areas. If "knows how to learn" has been identified as a desired skill, one question might be, "What can you think of that you taught yourself how to do?" Figure 3.5 lists possible questions for a maternal health position, based on the identified skills.

2. Consider other indicators for proof of the desired skills or attributes. It may be possible to detail other evidence of the skills identified through the job task analysis. For instance, com-

| | |
|---|---|
| 1. *Basic Skills:*<br>   Question: | reading; writing reports<br>What kind of reading do you most<br>enjoy? Why? |
| 2. *Higher Order Thinking:*<br>   Question: | knows how to learn<br>Tell me about anything you have taught<br>yourself to do. How did you do that?<br>If you were confronted with something<br>you didn't know how to do, what would<br>you do next? |
| 3. *Interpersonal:*<br>   Question: | empathizes; is sensitive to others<br>How would your best friends describe<br>you—in terms of how good a friend<br>you are? Why? |
| 4. *Communication:*<br>   Question: | is a good listener; a good speaker<br>Would your friends describe you as a<br>good listener? Why? Have you had<br>experience speaking in front of a group<br>of people? What was that like for you? |
| 5. *Personal Attributes:*<br>   Question: | is outgoing, friendly, motivated<br>How would you respond to a situation<br>where it appeared that a client did not<br>trust you or perhaps was immediately<br>afraid of you for some reason? |
| 6. *Knowledge/Experience:*<br>   Question: | has at least one child<br>What did you find most helpful to you<br>as a young mother in need of help?<br>Why? |
| 7. *Technical Skills:* | (none) |

**Figure 3.5**. Possible interview questions for a maternal-health counselor paraprofessional position.

ments on reference forms may be instructive. The application itself may reveal some indicators, although one should not rely on it for evidence of writing skills. Another writing indicator may be required if writing is a priority skill. Figure 3.6 illustrates how a skills-indicator checklist could be formulated to assist supervisors in assessing the appropriate skills during the interview process. Such a form could be copied to accompany each application.

3. Arrange the interview room for maximum safety. Supervisors may be interviewing people who have never been interviewed before or who have minimal experience with a formal interview. The interview setting should be designed to be as nonthreatening as possible. Applicants should be greeted by name and directed to a comfortable chair near the interviewer (not across the desk, opposite the interviewer). Conversation should commence in a easy manner while the interviewer begins to describe the position and its responsibilities. The applicant may be offered a paper and a pen for taking notes if needed. Putting the applicant at ease will improve the quality of the interview and allow the interviewer to listen and observe for the indicators of interest.

## CONDUCTING THE INTERVIEW

Although hiring decisions—even under the best of circumstances and with maximum preparation—are not going to be perfect, the process may be helped by employing two strategies in particular: asking open-ended questions and using strategic talk.

### Asking Open-ended Questions

Questions such as "Tell me about . . . ," "What do you think about . . . ," "How would you describe . . . " and "Why do you think . . . " encourage dialogue and reflection. After all, in order to listen for evidence of the skills identified as important, the supervisor must have substantially more than "yes" or

**Directions:**
Beside each skill, record the method of assessing the applicant's ability to perform the specific skill or his/her ability to
learn the skill through an initial training program. Examples of
methods of assessing skills include the application, observation
(during a group-information session), responses provided by references and the applicant's responses during the interview.
Next, indicate "yes" or "no" in the columns labeled "Current
Skill" and "Ability to Learn Skill."

Applicant Name: _____
Interviewer:        _____
Date:                 _____

---

| Skills Needed in Specific Paraprofessional Role | Method of Assessment | Current Skill? Yes/No | Ability to Learn Skill? Yes/No |
|---|---|---|---|
| 1. *Basic Academic*<br>   a. Reading<br>   b. Writing | | | |
| 2. *Higher Order Thinking*<br>   a. Learn how to learn<br>   b. Solve a problem | | | |
| 3. *Interpersonal*<br>   a. Empathizes<br>   b. Is sensitive to others | | | |
| 4. *Communication*<br>   a. Speaking<br>   b. Listening | | | |
| 5. *Personal Attributes*<br>   a. Friendly<br>   b. Outgoing | | | |
| 6. *Knowledge/Experience*<br>   a. Young mother<br>   b. Diabetes | | | |
| 7. *Technical*<br>   (none) | | | |

**Figure 3.6**. Formulating a skills-indicator checklist.

"no" answers. Using open-ended questions will help the interview become a two-way dialogue instead of a monologue by the interviewer.

Responding to open questions may be a matter of routine for the supervisor (the professional), but may prove a daunting task for the potential paraprofessional. If response is minimal at first, the question may be rephrased to elicit the desired response. It is good practice to pause a few extra seconds for a response if one is not immediately forthcoming. Another strategy is to use pictures or cards to spur conversation. For instance, six qualities of good listeners may be written on 3x5 cards (one per card). The cards are then displayed and the applicant asked to select one quality that best describes his or her own listening technique. The skillful interviewer will use that response to elicit further explanation by asking, "Why did you choose that particular listening skill? Please tell me about it." Such a strategy places some parameters on concepts that may otherwise be too difficult for applicants to simply start describing or discussing. Conducting an interview with an applicant who may have had little exposure to the highly verbal environment may require some creativity.

## Using Strategic Talk

Heyman (1994) recommends strategies that help us to avoid misunderstandings in communication. We believe these strategies have implications for interviewing applicants who have little work or interview experience. Heyman notes that misunderstandings come from a lack of shared context on both sides. To avoid putting someone in the position of having to be a mind reader, Heyman recommends using formulations, questions and answers, paraphrasing, examples and stories.

Heyman (1994) writes that "when we formulate talk we actually step outside the conversation and tell people what they should understand us to be saying in the conversation" (p. 38). Formulations work in both directions. An interviewer might begin with, "What I am going to ask you about now is in the area of teamwork." The respondent might say, "So what you're talking about is . . . " We say out loud our interpretation of the meaning of the talk. In this way, the understanding is not left to chance.

Heyman (1994) observes that questions and answers "go as far as language can go in telling us what people understand. What is clear and obvious to us may not always be clear and obvious to others" (p. 41). Questions demand answers and are a good tool for checking understanding. During the interview, the interviewer may ask, "What don't you understand about how I've just described the job?" The question should be posed in a way that tells the applicant questions are expected! Another interview question that may produce insight into how well the position is being understood is, "How do you see your skills fitting in with the job I've just described?"

When we translate what someone else has said into our own words, we are paraphrasing. This strategy affords the speaker an opportunity to determine if the talk has been understood. In the interview, an applicant's responses may be paraphrased by the interviewer and then followed by an open-ended question: "From what I've heard you say, you believe that you work really well with people. What would your friends say about that?"

To overcome some of the impreciseness of language, we can use examples. This strategy is particularly useful when interviewing paraprofessionals who may have little understanding of the position or of the circumstances in which they would find themselves. Pictures, audiotapes and videos may be used as examples. Again, placing parameters around otherwise ambiguous concepts is a wise strategy when interviewing applicants for paraprofessional positions.

"Let me tell you a story to show you what I mean" is a particularly valuable strategy when interviewing for paraprofessional positions. It places the topic in the context of the applicant. Stories should be simple, realistic, and within the applicant's frame of reference.

Strategic talk can go a long way toward setting parameters, reducing misunderstandings, and getting the kind of interview responses that lead to good hiring decisions. Obviously, planning interview questions takes analysis, creativity, and time.

## ADDITIONAL CONSIDERATIONS DURING THE INTERVIEW

Questions from candidates may be more in the form of "thinking out loud." They are working to place the interview into some framework and also to absorb a great deal of information. Their questions often pertain to exactly what they must do in order to accomplish the job. Examples include, "Would I be doing this by myself?" or "Do people want me to come into their homes?" or "Are they required to do this?"

Because they lack interview experience, applicants may be inclined to stray from the topic and become sidetracked, unaware that it is inappropriate to do so. Additionally, not knowing what kinds of questions to ask, they may launch into inquiries about salary and benefits—topics that are generally covered later in the interview process.

Applicants need to be told up front, when asked to respond to a certain situation, that their response is not a matter of right and wrong. Otherwise, they may respond and then ask, "Did I get it right?"

The challenge for the interviewer is to avoid being put off by what may seem to be inappropriate responses. It is more important that interviewers establish that the applicant has the basic skills, knowledge, and attitudes required to learn and do the job.

## AFTER EACH INTERVIEW IS COMPLETED

Following each individual interview, the interviewer should record additional notes and observations. It may be necessary to read the application again for details and references. The time to make a decision about an applicant is now. Typically, the interviewer at the point immediately following the interview will

have the strongest feelings about an applicant's (1) ability to perform the job; (2) motivation to do the job; and (3) likely "fit"
with the work environment.

## Yes, No, and Maybe

The interviewer should create three file folders, labeled
"Yes," "No," and "Maybe," if the number of applicants is fairly
great. Although hardly scientific as a method, this procedure is
extremely practical. If the evidence and feelings about an applicant are positive, the application should be placed in the "Yes"
folder immediately after the interview. If the applicant is clearly
not suited to the position, the application should be placed in
the "No" folder. If the applicant falls somewhere between the
two, the application should go into the "Maybe" folder.

After all the interviews have been conducted, the interviewer should return to the "Yes" folder for further consideration. If more "yes" applications than positions exist, applications then must be ranked. If not enough files exist in the "Yes"
folder to fill all the positions, the "Maybe" applicants should be
ranked and the top candidates should be added to the other top
candidates. At this point, applicants in the "No" folder should
be contacted and advised that they were not selected. It is not
wise to contact the "Maybe" applicants until the top applicants
have been offered positions and have accepted.

## Making the Offer

The interviewer will have learned at the very beginning of
the selection-and-hiring process how the actual hiring is to be
conducted. The interviewer may not have full authority to ex-
tend the job offer. The top applicants may be called back for a
second interview with another administrator or supervisor for
a final selection. Some administrators may simply want to review the applications and discuss the candidates with the origi-

nal interviewer. If an additional interview is required, administrative calendars should be cleared in advance to avoid delay.

## SUMMARY

Supervisors of programs that employ paraprofessionals want to recruit individuals who are motivated to do the work, who can do it, and who will fit in with the work environment. Of course, supervisors are still responsible for training paraprofessionals well enough to meet or exceed performance expectations. Time spent in carefully planning the selection-and-hiring process, however, will reap great program dividends and will free administrators to pursue new challenges — rather than later having to solve personnel problems that might have been avoided.

# CHAPTER 4

## Initial Training

A hotline operator for a state-run health care system for the poor was asked what kind of training she received for her job. "Someone showed me how to use the phone, suggested I start answering it, and write down any questions I had so we could go over them at the end of the day." When asked how she got through the day, she replied, "Every time I got a call, I put the person on hold and then shouted across the room, 'who knows the answer to . . . '!" (S. Madson, personal communication, January 6, 1997).

Unfortunately, this method of training is not unusual. Too often, job training for paraprofessionals consists of placing the new employee with a veteran employee and hoping the new one will catch on and the veteran will not run out of patience! This approach to training makes several often unwarranted assumptions, namely: (1) the employee with greater tenure does not mind doing the training; (2) the employee doing the training is a good trainer; (3) the work habits of the veteran employee are exemplary; (4) initial and consistent contact with the supervisor is not important; and (5) this method costs practically nothing and takes little or no time on the part of the supervisor.

We propose a far more comprehensive approach to training that will ultimately be rewarding to everyone involved. Our approach calls for a commitment to the development of paraprofessionals along the parallel dimensions of growth and competencies. It also requires a serious investment of time and thorough planning. When it is done correctly, initial training will result in employees who achieve higher levels of competency and outcomes than ever thought possible. It will also set the stage for continual program improvement.

For this discussion we assume that the initial training is the responsibility of the supervisor of the paraprofessionals in the field. (We recognize that some readers may not have that immediate responsibility but may supervise others who do or who will have it eventually.) This chapter begins with a brief discussion of special considerations for designing initial training programs for paraprofessionals. Then, orientation training is described in terms of both its importance and its content. The chapter next moves to a discussion of the necessity for providing a safe learning environment. Next, seven steps of planning are explained as they relate to designing the initial training. We then examine a performance appraisal instrument and discuss the relationship between performance expectations, the content of appraisals and the content of training. The chapter concludes with training enhancement strategies and the evaluation of the training.

## SPECIAL CONSIDERATIONS

Although it is unwise to stereotype paraprofessionals in any way in terms of what they bring to the work situation, we have learned through experience that certain factors should be recognized. For instance, paraprofessionals are not professionals. Quite often, paraprofessionals start a new position with only limited experience. They often lack the skills needed to transfer abstract ideas to specific situations. Moreover, they sometimes lack the skills to assert themselves in new situations. They've had little opportunity to develop their abilities.

Paraprofessionals usually have no formal training in any particular discipline. They probably do not bring a body of knowledge with them to the job. They must learn basic background knowledge if they are to be expected to make sound decisions and exercise good judgment concerning the information.

Training should be completed before work responsibilities are assumed. Supervisors sometimes make the mistake of wanting to see how new employees "work out" before investing too much time in training efforts. This strategy may be appropriate in the case of professionals but it is completely inappropriate for paraprofessionals. If they do not succeed it is probably because they were not adequately prepared for the tasks they were asked to perform. Paraprofessional productivity is directly related to the quality of the training provided, thereby making initial training a top priority.

Immediate supervisors must involve themselves with the paraprofessionals and their training if the training is provided by someone else. In some organizations, paraprofessionals are sent off to be trained by someone other than the immediate supervisor (for instance, at a regional training session). Sometimes initial training is conducted on-site, but not by the immediate supervisor. In both cases, we suggest three strategies to help the supervisor "connect" with the paraprofessionals' training: (1) Training objectives and planned activities should be reviewed thoroughly by the supervisor; (2) Supervisors should attend and participate in as much of the training as possible so that paraprofessionals will see that their supervisors attach value to the training and what they are being asked to learn; (3) Supervisors ought to plan for immediate, posttraining reinforcement of what the paraprofessionals learned and practiced.

## ORIENTATION TRAINING

Orientation training refers to the formal or informal sharing of information about the organization's policies and procedures. This training is typically provided by the organization's human resources department, is scheduled on a regular basis, and includes new employees from all departments. If this type of session is offered by the organization, supervisors should make every effort to attend a session and make note of the topics addressed before bringing in new employees. The next step is to determine what else new paraprofessionals need to know and to begin to plan for training that will address those needs. For instance, a generic orientation may include vacation-leave and sick-leave information, but may not detail how these forms of leave should be handled within a particular department.

If the organization does not offer a generic orientation program, supervisors will need to design and deliver one themselves. Orientation training should address the following topics: (1) business and working hours; (2) lunch hours and breaks; (3)) scheduling procedures, particularly for vacation and sick leave; (4) reimbursement procedures; (5) worker's compensation; (6) reports and records; (7) dress codes; (8) mission and goals of the organization; (9) office machinery, especially telephones and computers; (10) overtime/compensatory time; (11) employee benefits; and (12) parking.

Typical orientation programs are quite thorough in terms of explaining various benefits (such as medical and retirement benefits), but they are far less comprehensive about the day-to-day issues facing employees. The importance of these topics to paraprofessionals must not be underestimated, particularly concerning reimbursement of expenses.

## ESTABLISHING A SAFE
## LEARNING ENVIRONMENT

The ultimate success of any training model for paraprofessionals depends first and foremost on the establishment of learner safety in the learning environment. Most adult learners want to feel as safe in a learning environment as possible. According to Maslow (1968), a person's need to feel secure has to be met before the need to reach out and take risks can be realized. For adults who are not accustomed to being part of a learning group or who are uncertain of their abilities in a certain realm, the group-training experience may cause quite a bit of anxiety. If this concern is not taken into account, such anxiety and fear may have a negative impact on training results. Ironically, it may be the group experience that results in learner safety. Notes Silberman (1996), "one of the key ways to attain a feeling of safety and security is to be connected to other people and to feel included in a group" (p. 6).

Paraprofessionals in New England who were attending a multistate training conference were asked by a training facilitator to share in writing what made them feel unsafe in a learning environment (C. Giesecke, personal communication, May 8, 1997). Their responses were indicative of the need for the establishment of a safe learning environment when offering the initial training.

I do not feel safe when . . . :

- Everyone seems to know the answer but me.
- I am the only person in the group who is different.
- Everyone else seems to understand.
- I feel the others in the group are not like me, or if they think I am not like them.
- The teacher assumes everyone is familiar with the topic.
- I am in crowded spaces.
- Others laugh at me for asking a question—when they seem to think it should have been common sense knowledge.
- I am put on the spot.
- I don't have something and I hear, "Everyone has this!"
- I am in a group of people who are not my friends.

We recommend that supervisors do a learning needs assessment prior to training that will help them be aware of possible safety/comfort issues, many of which can be avoided with preparation. Three questions might be asked of participants—if not all of them, then a representative sample:

- What experiences have you had in other training programs?
- What are your expectations of this training program?
- What are your concerns about this training?

We believe it is important to approach the initial training design with a good sense of what the learners need and expect. Supervisors should keep in mind that for the new paraprofessionals up to this point, their experience with the new organization has been primarily a solo one. Initial training often requires group involvement so issues of learner safety must be addressed.

## THE SEVEN STEPS OF PLANNING

Vella (1994, 1995) proposes a seven-step planning model that we find useful when designing everything from training programs to staff meetings. Following the model requires us to analyze what we are doing, what we are expecting, and for what we will be held accountable. The seven steps are Who, Why, When, Where, What, What For, and How.

### Who?

Who will participate in the training? In this case, the answer is recently hired human service paraprofessionals. Other information about the participants (such as age, cultural background, parenting experience, and language proficiency) might have a significant impact on the training design. Also considered in the "Who" step is the number of people to be trained. Group size has a major influence on the training design and on what may be accomplished.

### Why?

In "Why," we specify the situation that calls for the training. For this discussion, the training is required so that newly hired paraprofessionals may practice the skills they need to perform their jobs at a minimally acceptable level of competence. Initial training, although it should set the stage for growth and development, is first and foremost designed to teach basic job task competencies. A strong foundation of competencies provides the groundwork for future development.

## When?

Initial training should be conducted immediately after the paraprofessionals are hired. It is the supervisor's responsibility to ensure that all schedules are well coordinated and that training commences immediately. The "When" also includes the overall training schedule. Other factors to consider that are incorporated into the "When" step are time of year and time of day issues. An example of the "When" affecting training is when training takes place just as a school year is starting. It will be quite difficult for some new paraprofessionals to negotiate both events at once if they have school-age children.

## Where?

The "Where" of any training is critically important and can affect the entire design, time frame, numbers served, and continuity. Is sufficient space available for both seating and learning activities? Is the space user-friendly? Is the lighting adequate? Is the space available for a sufficient length of time for the training to be conducted and completed? Is the space situated near other training rooms where unrelated activities and noises may compete for the trainees' attention?

## What?

The "What" is at the very heart of the training program. It is the actual content. Technically speaking, the content of the training should be derived from the performance appraisal instrument (if one exists). The first question to ask is, "Upon what standard are employees going to be evaluated?" The second question should be, "How will we design a training program that allows new paraprofessionals to meet those standards?" (An actual performance appraisal instrument is included in Appendix A and the 4-week training that matches it is included in Appendix B). These identified competencies become the basis of the "What" step or the content of the initial training program. We will continue our discussion of the relationship between the performance appraisal instrument and training content after addressing the remaining two planning steps.

## What For?

With the content established, the next step is to determine what participants will achieve as a result of the training, or what they will do with the content. The "What For" step may be regarded as determining the training objectives. Broadly viewed, the overall training objective is for participants to have practiced and applied the competencies they need to successfully perform the job tasks. The training objectives should be achievement based. The overall long-term training objectives should be achievement based as well, so that the supervisor can measure the quality and results of the training. Examples of achievement-based objectives during the initial training include, "Participants will have practiced asking open-ended questions of one another," and, "Participants will have analyzed six strategies for recruiting new clients into the program." An example of a long-term achievement-based objective is, "Within twelve months of completion of the orientation and training program, paraprofessionals will graduate 75% of participants within 6 months of enrollment." The results may be observed and quantified.

## How?

The seventh of the seven steps of planning is the "How." This step answers the question, "How will the participants accomplish the achievement-based objectives?" For instance, if the objective is for participants to analyze six strategies for recruiting new families into the program, exactly how will they accomplish this? The "How" is where learning tasks are designed that pose a problem or ask a question of the learners. They are given the necessary materials and content to respond.

Figure 4.1 illustrates a lesson that we developed using the

| | |
|---|---|
| WHO: | The six new paraprofessionals receiving initial training. |
| WHY: | They must be knowledgeable enough of every unit in the required curriculum to both teach it and have command of the nutrition and meal planning concepts that learners need to know. |
| WHEN: | Fourth day of training, afternoon session, approximately 1:00 to 4:30. |
| WHERE: | Cooperative Extension demonstration kitchen. |
| WHAT: | "Planning Makes the Difference" lesson. |
| WHAT FOR: | By the end of this session, participants will have |

  1. Compared grocery store advertisements and determined the best food buys.
  2. Planned meals for a week, utilizing best food buys and meeting dietary requirements.
  3. Analyzed their role as the teacher instead of the participant.

HOW:  Task 1: For a warm-up, participants will name the best buy they have found while grocery shopping.

Task 2: Current grocery store advertisements will be distributed to each participant. They will be asked to identify good food buys. They will then share them with the group and the trainer will lead a discussion and create a master list of good food buys.

Task 3: Using the master list of good food buys, participants work in pairs to plan meals for one week utilizing the food they have on hand and the good food buys whenever possible. The meals must also meet the dietary guidelines of the Food Guide Pyramid.

Task 4: Participants share the meals they planned with the group, as well as their frustrations or difficulties in meeting the dietary requirements.

Task 5: Participants create a grocery list of the items needed to prepare the meals they have planned. (Participants should be reminded not to include the items they already have on hand.)

Task 6: Participants are challenged to identify substitutions for their planned meals if resources do not allow them to purchase all the items needed.

Task 7: Participants are asked to brainstorm possible difficulties associated with teaching this lesson. Experienced paraprofessionals should be available to address concerns and offer suggestions.

**Figure 4.1.** Planning makes the difference.

seven steps of planning and achievement-based objectives. We envision that the initial training for paraprofessionals will contain a series of lessons similar to our example, "Planning Makes the Difference." This particular lesson is part of Baker's (1994) 4-week paraprofessional training program for nutrition program assistants, which is located in Appendix B.

Readers will note that the lesson objectives are not written in terms of "will be able to," "will have knowledge of," or "will have learned." Each objective represents something participants will do with lesson content during the training and an observable achievement.

## THE PERFORMANCE APPRAISAL INSTRUMENT

As stated earlier, the content of an initial training program ideally should be derived from the performance appraisal instrument. We believe such an instrument deserves more discussion here because of the specialized nature of training paraprofessionals. If the organization utilizes a standard performance appraisal document, the supervisor should determine if it is appropriate to use with paraprofessionals. We offer six key questions supervisors should ask about a performance appraisal instrument:

1. Is the performance appraisal specific to the job tasks?

2. Does it assess specific job performance standards?

3. Is it written in language paraprofessionals will relate to (for example, the language you use with them)?

4. Does it address all the items mentioned in the job description?

5. Does it incorporate a mechanism that allows the supervisor to rank paraprofessionals? (The answer to this question could be important if merit increases are awarded.)

6. Does it include a mechanism for assessing progress toward previous goals and for goal setting for the future?

If a performance appraisal form is not already developed, or if the form in use is not specific to the tasks performed, a job specific form should be developed. If a program is so new that a performance appraisal instrument does not yet exist, training content can be derived from the job task analysis discussed in Chapter 2. Our sample performance appraisal is located in Appendix A.

The paraprofessionals evaluated by our sample instrument deliver food and nutrition education to low-income families. The first page of the instrument defines minimum performance standards and performance expectations. It also provides spaces for an overall rating and for signatures. The major categories to be evaluated include (1) quantity of work; (2) quality of work; (3) work habits; (4) relations with others; (5) work attitudes; (6) evaluating progress toward last year's goal; and (7) goal-setting for the next year.

## Areas to Address in Initial Training Based on The Instrument

Although the specific areas addressed in each of these categories will be different for each paraprofessional position, the major categories are typical to most performance evaluation instruments. Evaluating progress toward last year's goals and setting goals for next year are important to performance evaluation, but not critical for the initial training. Most often, the goals relate to the first five categories. Supervisors, using the performance appraisal instrument, can design training activities to address each of the competencies (areas addressed in each category of the instrument). We briefly examine each one in terms of human service paraprofessionals.

Quantity of work is the area that most people expect to be evaluated on, and paraprofessionals are no different. The performance expectations related to quantity of work should be addressed in the initial training. Paraprofessionals will need clarity on expectations. Where "quantity of work" refers to "how much," "quality of work" refers to "how well." We have found that balancing the two—quantity and quality—is quite challenging for paraprofessionals.

Work habits should be included in initial training for inexperienced paraprofessionals. They simply do not know what is expected of them. We include time management, scheduling, planning, use of time, interpersonal skills, and reporting procedures in this category. Concepts that professionals with work experience may take for granted, such as being on time for work, calling if one is going to be late, and planning in advance for leave time, may be foreign to some paraprofessionals.

As discussed in Chapter 2, relations with others may be the premiere skill or quality desired in a paraprofessional. Building and maintaining relationships may be quite difficult for some new paraprofessionals whose experience has been only with family and friends. New relationships include ones with coworkers, supervisors, administrators, clients, and people from other agencies. The paraprofessionals will need to be skilled at developing these relationships if they are to be successful with their work. Therefore, the initial training should address relationship building.

The category of work attitudes measures the level of initiative that a paraprofessional brings to improvement of job performance. It also measures how well the individual responds to direction from the supervisor. These expectations should be specifically addressed in the initial training. Experience in welfare reform has already taught us that some people, particularly young women who have been in sole charge of a household and a child, have difficulty accepting supervision and criticism and may perceive these as disrespect. Supervisors will want to address work attitude forthrightly in initial training, using clear language and clear expectations.

Figure 4.2 represents an overview of 1 week of an actual, 4-week training program. We realize that training program length will vary from situation to situation. At the same time, the training program referred to here has proven highly effective.

The performance appraisal areas addressed during the first week include Quality of Work, Quantity of Work, Relations With Others and Work Attitudes.

*Day 1*
 Module 1:  Orientation to Organization/Job
 Module 2:  EFNEP Roles and Extension Relationships
------------------------------------------------------------------
*Day 2*
 Module 3:  Introduction to Eating Right is Basic 2
            (the curriculum)
 Module 4:  Making Meals from What's on Hand
------------------------------------------------------------------
*Day 3*
 Module 5:  Nutrients We Need
 Module 6:  Planning Makes The Difference
------------------------------------------------------------------
*Day 4*
 Module 7:  Shopping Basics
 Module 8:  Let's Make Something Simple
------------------------------------------------------------------
*Day 5*
 Module 9:  Observation/Practice Enrolling with Experienced
            NPA (nutrition program assistant)

**Figure 4.2.** An Overview of Unit 1—the first week. Designed for paraprofessionals working with the Expanded Food and Nutrition Program
for the Cooperative Extension Service (Baker, 1994).


Figure 4.3 represents the specific content outline for the
first week rather than just the overview. This outline should help
readers continue to envision the process for determining initial
training content. Readers should note that the orientation training is included in Week One of the overall paraprofessional
training, rather than standing alone.

Quality of work (content areas including specific topics,
subject matter and mission), quantity of work (enrollment procedures), relations with others (on-the-job observation) and work
attitudes (on-the-job observation) are specifically addressed in
the modules. Modules three through eight are actual lessons in
the EFNEP curriculum. During the initial training new paraprofessionals first play the role of learner and then discuss their
role as the teacher of these lessons. Module 9 allows each new
paraprofessional to spend a day observing a tenured paraprofes-

EFNEP ORIENTATION
Unit 1—Content Outline

Module 1:  Orientation to Organization/Job (3 hours)
           A. Employee Benefits
           B. Pretest
           C. EFNEP questionnaire
           D. Extension's mission, vision and goals
Module 2:  EFNEP Roles and Extension Relationship (3 hours)
           A. History of Extension/land-grant institutions
           B. Administrative chain-of-command
           C. Subject matter specialists
           D. History of EFNEP
           E. Program assistants' role in county staff
           F. *The Mission of the EFNEP Program Assistant* (video)
Module 3:  Introduction to *Eating right is Basic 2* (2 hours).
           A. Participants receive curriculum
           B. Determining client eligibility
           C. Client enrollment procedures
Module 4:  Making Meals from What's On Hand (3 hours).
           A. Meal planning
           B. Food selection
           C. Food preparation
Module 5:  Nutrients We Need (3 hours)
           A. Introduction to nutrition
           B. *How Food Affects Us* (slide/tape)
           C. *Nutrition in the Life Cycle* (video)
           D. Food preparation
Module 6:  Planning Makes a Difference (3 hours)
           A. Meal planning as part of a healthy diet
           B. Meal planning
           C. Food selection
           D. Food storage
           E. Food preparation
Module 7:  Shopping Basics (3 hours)
           A. Meal planning
           B. Food selection
           C. Food storage
           D. Food preparation

**Figure 4.3.** First week content outline for the expanded food and nutrition program paraprofessionals. (Baker, 1994)

Module 8:   Let's Make Something Simple (2 hours, 30 minutes)
            A. Meal planning
            B. Food selection
            C. Food preparation
Module 9:   Observation/Practice Enrolling With Experienced NPA (6
            hours)
            A. Complete *Observation of Teaching Visit* form
            B. Look for:
                1. Teaching techniques
                2. Recruitment techniques
                3. NPA relationship with participants

**Figure 4.3.** First week content outline for the expanded food and nutrition program paraprofessionals. (Baker, 1994) (continued)

sional at work. In the EFNEP model developed by Baker (1994), these on-the-job opportunities are part of every week of training. They should be incorporated early in the training so that new paraprofessionals can see right away how their training relates to what they will be doing once the training is complete. It also helps them reinforce what they are learning in training. The new paraprofessionals prepare for the practice days and reflect upon what they observe and learn.

The entire training outline by Baker (1994) is located in Appendix B. Readers should note that it requires all 4 weeks of the initial training to adequately cover the five work areas—(1) quantity of work, (2) quality of work, (3) work habits, (4) work attitudes, and (5) relations with others.

## STRATEGIES TO ENHANCE PARAPROFESSIONAL TRAINING

Several strategies may be employed by trainers of paraprofessionals that should enhance training outcomes. Although these strategies are appropriate for training in general, they are especially important for paraprofessionals because of the relative lack of experience they bring to their positions.

Initial training programs should open with activities that build respect and safety. Trainers should take plenty of time to get a good start, putting learners at ease, helping them become comfortable with the concept of working with so many other people, giving them an opportunity to become acquainted with the other trainees, and allowing them to experience immediate success. The temptation will be to move too quickly, to design a quick "warm-up" and keep moving. A warm-up should always be part of the overall content and it should not be rushed. It is not a game. It is the foundation upon which all else will thrive or struggle. It is the beginning of respect and safety and ultimately of learning.

A strategy we have used successfully on the first day of training to enhance respect and safety is to design the room so that it anticipates the learners. A name tent may be set at every place to welcome its namesake. Folders and notebooks should be placed at everyone's seat with, names embossed. Pencils, pens, and notepads should be arranged for everyone. Participants in the training will see immediately that they are both expected and honored.

Each content area should be developed as part of a spiral curriculum, with each part connecting to the next part and with the level of difficulty increasing. Throughout the "spiral effect," participants will get to practice not just new skills but ones they have already experienced. Adult learners can become frustrated quickly if they either do not see the relationship between two components of training or perceive they are falling behind other participants.

Content areas need to be addressed in a manner that allows participants to ground topics in their own experiences, discuss and analyze new information, apply the new knowledge and skills, and synthesize what they have learned. Trainers should want participants to see and understand the material that is being taught is related to their lives and work.

Training activities should be based on dialogue instead of monologue, with three components of a learning activity represented: content, action, and reflection. Each activity should include information, something that may be done with the information, and some opportunity to reflect upon what was learned. Facilitators may make ample use of open-ended questions and learner participation. We point out that dialogue is not the same as a question-and-answer session. During "Q and A," participants ask questions of the trainer or offer ideas and the trainer essentially listens, clarifies, or paraphrases their comments. Designing for dialogue, by distinction, involves participants exchanging ideas among themselves, giving meaning to what they are learning, and shaping it with their own experiences and perspectives. Although question-and-answer sessions are quite valuable, we encourage readers to go beyond that format and allow the participants to generate questions and answers among themselves.

To help readers understand what needs to happen in a training environment in relation to dialogue, we offer the concept of Levels of Interaction.

Levels of Interaction in a Training Environment

| | |
|---|---|
| Level 1: | The trainer speaks and participants listen. |
| Level 2: | The trainer speaks and participants are invited to pose questions, if any, to the trainer. |
| Level 3: | The trainer speaks and asks participants to address a content based question with a partner. The pair will be asked to report on their responses. |
| Level 4: | Identical to Level 3, except that the two people involved in the discussion are asked to offer their comments or factors, both in writing and aloud, so that everyone else can see (or hear) them. |
| Level 5: | Identical to Level 4, except that in each group there are more than two involved in the discussion. |

Clearly, we can generate any number of variations on Levels of Interaction, including one in which the trainer does not speak but could instead show a video or do a demonstration.

The important point is what participants do with the content, regardless of how it is presented. As the readers may recall, our training approach is based on achievement objectives which require that participants do something with the information they receive. Training should be designed to utilize, at minimum, Level 3 interactions as often as possible. As Silberman (1996) notes, we do not learn simply by having content presented to us. We learn by considering it and talking about it. He makes the distinction between the brain as a videotape recorder (which it is not) and the brain as a processor of information, always asking questions, always seeking patterns and meanings. To enhance training outcomes for paraprofessionals, those designing and conducting the training should provide ample opportunities for participants to process information.

Finally, training activities should be designed around the idea of learning by doing. Vella (1994) utilizes the concept of adult learners remembering 20% of what they hear, 40% of what they see, and 80% of what they see, hear and do. Readers may examine the tasks that are described in Figure 4.1 to see how participants will be actively engaged in dialogue and will be learning by doing.

## EVALUATING THE INITIAL TRAINING

### Summative Evaluation

The training program may be evaluated summatively by referring to the training objectives envisioned for a year. Figure 4.4 illustrates the 12-month objectives of the EFNEP Paraprofessional Orientation and Training Program, which are stated in terms of achievement.

The levels of achievement may be examined at monthly intervals so that supervisors will know what areas of competency should be addressed in ongoing training or will know what to improve for future initial training.

- Organize the recommended minimum number of groups.
- Maintain a minimum of 20 enrolled homemakers 80% of the time.
- Achieve improved diets as indicated by EFNEP dietary recalls and scores on EFNEP Exit Surveys with 85% of the clients.
- Graduate 75% of homemakers within 6 months of their enrollment.
- Achieve minimum job performance standards (66 teaching visits per month) three out of four months.
- Accurately report clients' demographic information on dietary and survey responses.
- Design lesson plans based on learners' needs and nutrition subject matter.
- Achieve minimum proficiency in teaching methods and strategies.

**Figure 4.4.** Objectives of the EFNEP paraprofessional orientation and training program, within 12 months of completion.


## Formative Evaluation

Evaluation and feedback are important elements of any training session, but they are especially important to extensive training programs which build knowledge and skills. However, it is also important that paraprofessionals not feel they are continually being tested. We have used a variety of strategies to evaluate participants' performance and learning during training without having to administer pen-and-paper tests. For instance, after specific segments of teaching new material, participants should be invited to ask questions that will reflect their new level of understanding and their ability to apply the information to specific situations.

Trainers will want to ask frequent open-ended questions and employ strategies that literally invite questions. For instance, participants can be given a supply of index cards and encouraged to jot down their questions or concerns on the cards, placing them in a basket at their own discretion. Learners need not sign their names on the cards. Trainers may periodically review the questions, answer them, and adjust the training activities, if needed.

After introducing new skills, participants should be provided with the opportunity to practice those skills in a safe environment. The level of competence displayed by participants will inform the trainer if additional time is required or if changes in program design are warranted.

The specific objectives for each training segment should be reviewed at the conclusion of each segment. As a group, the participants and the trainer may decide if objectives have been met and if additional time should be spent on particular topics.

Formal evaluation opportunities are also important, and a pen-and-paper test may be one way to assess transfer of knowledge. We recommend, however, that this strategy be combined with observation of practice sessions, demonstrations, role plays, and on-the-job activities.

## ALTERNATIVE TRAINING ARRANGEMENTS

Our strategies and examples have assumed that one person is responsible for both designing and conducting the training. However, supervisors do have other options, including sharing the training responsibilities.

What happens if one person cannot do all the training? A trainer may be responsible for the training design and the overall implementation of the training, but may not feel well versed in every topic. Another person may be invited to conduct a particular training segment. Although this arrangement can be very effective, all presenters must know their audience. They must be skilled at taking broad or abstract principles and applying them to specific situations that paraprofessionals will encounter on the job. With proper training, support, and practice, paraprofessionals will improve in their application of abstract principles, but the initial training experience should remain as concrete as possible.

The supervisor, when present at training sessions conducted by guests, has the opportunity to observe paraprofessionals and assess their understanding, questions, responses, and reactions. Often the supervisor can interject a clarifying statement or pose questions that no one else may feel comfortable in asking. The mere presence of the supervisor may serve to endorse the content being presented as well as to assist in providing an environment in which new staff can participate comfortably.

What happens if the supervisor has access to funds but does not immediately have the time or skills necessary to develop and/or deliver a thorough initial training program? The work may be contracted to an outside trainer, provided that those who are contracted with have a thorough understanding of what the program is to accomplish, the special training needs of paraprofessionals, and the supervisor's commitment to collaboration.

Another option is to use the training guide of a similar program and adapt it to the needs of the organization. Those who are responsible for providing training for paraprofessionals may proceed with this strategy and over a period of time make adaptations that allow for a more complete fit between the "borrowed" approach and the immediate needs of the program.

## SUMMARY

However the initial training program is developed, its worth will be demonstrated time and again as program outcomes are met and paraprofessionals develop in their abilities and increase their levels of confidence. We have made references in this volume to the commitment, time, and planning required to maximize paraprofessional potential. A well-designed initial training program, while requiring great quantities of all three, will be well worth the investment.

# CHAPTER 5

## Supported Transition

Whether the initial training was designed and conducted by the supervisor, or whether the supervisor had outside help (or perhaps sent the paraprofessionals elsewhere for training), the supervisor's most important role is just now beginning. At this point, paraprofessionals must be guided along a skills—and—confidence continuum, picking up where the initial training left them. We refer to this phase as supported transition. As with all previous steps of the model, from analysis to selection to training, this fourth component requires time and planning. This chapter addresses the need for a strong supported transition period and then outlines specific strategies.

### REASONS FOR SUPPORTED TRANSITION

#### Change Is Just the Beginning

Let us consider the following hypothetical situation. It is Friday afternoon and Dora has just completed her first week as a teacher's aide in a Head Start program. If anyone had asked her at that moment how she felt about her new job, she might have said, "Oh, I'm already loving it!" But she could have said much more. "I never dreamed what taking this job would cost me in terms of my personal life. I never heard anything in training about how I feel right now. I'm not sure this is worth it."

Dora is a single mother with a three-year-old daughter, Karla. Until now, she has taken care of her daughter by herself, with occasional help from a neighbor or friend. Now she and Karla are up before dawn, fussing and fighting to get dressed, eat breakfast, and get to the daycare center. Although Karla seems all right, Dora doesn't really trust the daycare center, and she misses her daughter. Come to think of it, everything is different now. Dora previously had time for her friends and they would talk about things they had in common. Now her friends act differently toward her. Dora must dress for work every day and add new clothes to her budget. A week ago, it all seemed so exciting. Today, it just seems lonely.

Bridges (1991), would not be surprised at Dora's predicament or with our failure to notice it. He draws a useful distinction between change and transition. Change is what is new—a move, a reorganization, a new baby, a new job, a first job—but it is just the catalyst for what is to follow. Transition begins with endings, because with every change one must let go of old behaviors and routines.

Now let us consider what newly hired human service paraprofessionals may be letting go, keeping in mind that this may be their first real job, their first real salary plus benefits. What may be ending?

- Social time with friends and family;
- Staying home with a child;
- Not needing an alarm clock;
- Wearing whatever one wants;
- Not needing steady transportation;
- Reading just for fun;
- Flexibility in scheduling;
- Favorite television shows which were discussed with friends;
- Getting meals together at any time;
- Answering only to one's self.

And what might be replacing what was lost?

- Having to be constantly learning something new;
- Always being evaluated and compared;
- Being anxious about time and schedules;
- Having to wear a watch;

- Having to drive, perhaps for much greater distances;
- Being supervised;
- Always meeting strangers;
- Having someone else spend weekdays with one's child.

Many paraprofessionals will have to adjust to being paid monthly instead of nothing at all or weekly. Although dealing with transportation and childcare are difficult even for professionals, these issues can bring absolute despair to paraprofessionals who often do not have sufficient finances or backup to handle crises. In a Chicago hospital-based breastfeeding intervention program, paraprofessionals were hired to do the client counseling (Kistin, Abramson, & Dublin, 1994). Project coordinators, in hindsight, learned that they had greatly underestimated the time they would need to spend supporting the paraprofessionals through their personal problems, such as finances, cars, childcare, relationships, and illnesses. Coordinators realized that the lives of their outreach workers were as prone to crisis as the lives of their clients.

Perhaps the greatest loss for the paraprofessionals, ironically, will ultimately turn into greatest gain—a sense of competence. They may have felt quite competent and secure in their lives before the new job and find themselves now facing new uncertainties every day. With proper training and supported transition, however, they may eventually develop a new sense of competence that will take them to higher levels in their careers and within their own families. Their new sense of competence will become apparent in program outcomes as well.

## Loss of Anonymity

We mentioned that the new paraprofessional now has to learn constantly and be evaluated while doing it. Supervisors may believe that learning issues were already handled by the time the initial training is completed. After all, they looked for basic skills indicators in the selection process and then designed achievement-based training. What must be remembered, however, is that the initial training was accomplished in a warm, comfortable environment among very supportive people. The real world is altogether different.

Chesterton (1995), referring to training hourly employees, noted the reliance of many people on concealment strategies, that is, finding ways to get other people to do certain learning tasks for them. He noted employees' fears of having to read aloud, having to read a passage silently and then respond to it in writing within a certain time frame, having to speak in public, or having their poor language skills exposed. One of the authors of this volume spoke to a group of nutrition paraprofessionals several years ago and noticed a young woman patiently waiting for everyone else to leave the room so she could speak to the presenter. "You said you've done work in literacy education. Could you help me? I have a terrible learning disability and have to get by all the time at my job. I've never told anyone about it." (H. Lane, personal communication, November 1, 1993). Supervisors should assume that some paraprofessionals have utilized concealment strategies in the past and will find their new exposure to evaluation very frightening. Supported transition, therefore, is critical to successful outcomes.

## Managing Multiple Tasks

Supervisors look for multiple task management ability during the interviews and in their interactions with paraprofessionals during training. Nevertheless, new paraprofessionals are often overwhelmed as they begin their job tasks. One paraprofessional who participated in a training session conducted by the authors described it this way: "How I have wanted to get into a program like this, and now it all comes at once and there is not enough time in the day to get it all done. I guess I am not up to this." (M. Pearson, personal communication, April 23, 1996).

This type of reaction is not necessarily an indication that people received less-than-adequate orientation and training. It simply means they are struggling to simultaneously do all the things they have learned. In the training program, they probably learned new skills individually, such as, data collection, interviewing, and teaching. On the job, however, all the skills they learned may be called for at the same time. Suddenly the scenario is real life. That stress alone may cause paraprofessionals to freeze or forget much of what they learned in training.

Paraprofessionals also face distractions on the job that did not exist in the training room. Clients may be rude or hurried or, as outreach workers so often find, they may pretend not to be home when the paraprofessional knocks on the door or rings the bell. Other examples include a loud television, small children crying, the telephone ringing, or the supervisor or another experienced paraprofessional observing. Supported transition, from training through the first weeks on the job, can help eliminate (or at least diffuse) the dreaded feeling of being overwhelmed.

## Working Within a Group

Human service paraprofessionals are expected not only to deal with clients all day, but also to blend harmoniously with each other. Feedback received by the authors at various paraprofessional training workshops reveals that this expectation can be quite difficult, particularly for the newest people. One of the authors had just completed a 2-day training session with 35 paraprofessionals when she was waved over to a table by a woman perhaps in her thirties. "I really enjoyed everything we did here and I'm going to use these new teaching techniques when I get back home. But let me ask you: do you do training that would help us all get along at our own office? We need that more than anything." (M. Brown, personal communication, July 18, 1995).

During the job task analysis, selection process, and initial training, supervisors looked for interpersonal skills and an overall fit with the program. In spite of their best efforts, however, it would rarely be enough to ensure mere inner office harmony — never mind teamwork. Paraprofessionals may never before have been required to get along with so many people. They may demonstrate behaviors that worked well in their previous lives but are disastrous now. Supervisors should be cognizant of group-related issues and not assume that the new paraprofessionals will all move into the new work environment with ease.

## STRATEGIES FOR SUPPORTED TRANSITION

We have focused on the paraprofessionals themselves in terms of their need for strong, supported transition. Perhaps the greatest reason for the support is program potential. Paraprofessionals are hired to work with certain audiences because of the presumption that they can do a better job of it than professionals. And so they can, but not overnight. Supervisors have several strategies at their disposal to ensure that a strong, supported transition is both provided for and successfully completed by the new paraprofessionals.

### Learn What Paraprofessionals Do

Feedback over the years from paraprofessionals indicates that they do not believe their supervisors really know what they face each day. Some supervisors rarely—if ever—go out with their employees on client calls or spend the day in a clinic or a classroom, except for the purpose of observing or evaluating. Sometimes supervisors do not want to go where their paraprofessionals go (for instance, to public housing communities, back country roads, shanties with outhouses, community centers at night, or homeless shelters). A paraprofessional who was participating in a workshop facilitated by one of the authors expressed her feelings of isolation. "People sit back and say that we have an easy job. But even though we do work part-time, the job is not easy. We don't just go and teach nutrition to our people. We hear and understand their very own personal problems. Half the time our supervisor does not even recognize us

or see what we do. I'm tired of not being seen. I feel invisible."
(K. Layton, personal communication, October 30, 1996).

The crux of this strategy—learning what paraprofessionals do—is respect. Paraprofessionals are quick to recognize their supervisors' reluctance to accompany them into the field and easily translate it into not respecting what they do. Perhaps more so, the supervisor's absence may signal a significant lack of understanding of the paraprofessional's failures. After all, how can the supervisor understand not just the successes but also the failures when he or she has spent so little time in actual work situations?

The authors have interacted with hundreds of human service paraprofessionals in a program that delivers nutrition education to limited-resource audiences. Far surpassing all reported problems is that of clients who fail to keep appointments. The "cousins" of this problem are (1) a client being genuinely surprised that an appointment had been scheduled when the paraprofessional appears; or (2) a client attending one group session and then failing to attend the rest. The ultimate perplexity that everyone dislikes is when a client is at home but hides behind a curtain and refuses to answer the door.

These events are taken personally by new human service paraprofessionals who struggle to do everything so well and are undone by such perceived rejection. Supervisors may be aware of these problems, but do they really know what it feels like? Are their own empathy indicators working? In order to know and to feel, supervisors must experience the world of their paraprofessionals on some regular basis. The paraprofessionals need to know that their supervisors are taking into account both the joys and the heartbreaks of their work. If paraprofessionals are telephone hotline workers, then the supervisor could take a turn on the switchboard from time to time. If they are immunization outreach workers for a managed-care company working with Medicaid-eligible clients, the supervisor could periodically accompany them on home visits. To respect and be respected, supervisors must experience firsthand what their paraprofessionals experience.

## Develop a Relationship with Each Paraprofessional

Supervisors must work within their own time limitations and obligations to other duties. However, they also need to make time for developing relationships with new paraprofessionals. To admit their fears and insecurities about performing the job, paraprofessionals must feel a high level of trust in the supervisor. This trusting relationship begins in the interview process and continues throughout the orientation and initial training. If the supervisor is not the primary trainer, the trusting relationship still must be built. Informal interaction is also important. Having lunch with the new paraprofessional and discussing non-work-related topics will show the supervisor's interest in the paraprofessional as a person as well as an employee.

Supervisors often find themselves saying, "Why didn't you ask?" Instead, however, they should be asking themselves, "What could I have done differently so that this person would have felt comfortable asking?" Supervisors could structure the first days of the transition period to include individual interaction with each new paraprofessional. For example, the supervisor might ask each new employee to come by the office near the end of the day to discuss that day's events. If this type of office arrangement does not apply, the supervisor should still provide opportunities for informal coaching and feedback with new people on an individual basis. If the supervisor structures the first important days of the transition period to include individual interaction, the paraprofessionals will likely assume that this type of dialogue is acceptable and encouraged.

It may be useful to think in terms of *task* and *relationship*, and to consider these concepts as a ratio. In the early stages of new paraprofessionals' work, supervisors should think: *high relationship to low task*. It will certainly take an appreciable amount of time for some newly hired people to master the tasks of the job and then to meet or exceed performance of expectations, but initially the supervisory emphasis should be on developing the relationship. By so doing, the new paraprofessional becomes receptive to listening, learning, and asking questions. A trusting relationship precedes the teaching relationship.

Later, as the task component increases, the relationship time-investment will diminish. Eventually, the supervisor will be able to think: *low relationship to high task*, but may return to the original ratio of *high relationship to low task* should performance become an issue.

## Combine Support With Challenge

During the first few days on the job, paraprofessionals should be able to approach the supervisor and get the answers they need. Gradually, they should be involved in formulating the answers to their questions, and ultimately they should seek verification that they have arrived at appropriate solutions. If these steps are not taken gradually as part of coaching the new employee, the paraprofessional may develop a false sense of dependence on the supervisor. It is the supervisor's role to begin challenging the employees to solve problems themselves.

## Provide Immediate Positive Feedback

When paraprofessionals initiate interactions on their own, they ought to receive positive feedback for their efforts. Even if a suggestion is not appropriate, the paraprofessional should be praised for initiative and encouraged to bring other ideas and comments. A simple response such as, "That's a very good question!" can be the encouragement that an insecure paraprofessional needs to keep trying. If paraprofessionals perceive that their supervisors are not interested in their input or questions, they will be less likely to come forward again.

Supervisors should look for positive things to commend about the paraprofessionals' performance. It may be a job task that the paraprofessional struggled with during training but is now performing at expectation on the job. Even when mistakes are made or performance does not yet meet expectations, supervisors can point out improvements and other areas where performance is good. Success should be experienced quickly! Even a small success may provide sufficient motivation to overcome a mistake or frustration.

Opportunities to celebrate should never be missed. Simply completing the initial training is cause for celebration. The feeling of success that results from completing the training may be the encouragement the new paraprofessional needs to manage the transition. The supervisor may award certificates of achievement and invite other administrators and other tenured paraprofessionals to participate. Perhaps the greatest supervisor/ trainer role with paraprofessionals is to continually promote and celebrate learning.

## Place New Paraprofessionals with Experienced Ones

It is not unusual for paraprofessionals to be unsure of their abilities, some more than others. Struggling paraprofessionals must see beyond a doubt that their supervisors believe in them. It may be helpful for paraprofessionals who are experiencing particularly difficult transitions to spend time with exemplary, more seasoned employees. It can be very reassuring to hear from others who do the job very well about their own first, anxious days. Often the experienced person more easily becomes a role model for the new employee than does the supervisor. The important message to communicate to paraprofessionals who are struggling is that problems will be conquered together and that they will eventually learn to solve problems on their own.

## Build a Solid Foundation of Respect and Safety

All people want to be respected for who they are, where they have been and what they know. The "fraternal twin," so to speak, of respect, is safety. It carries the same degree of significance but with its own identity. Without an atmosphere of safety paraprofessionals simply will not perform as their supervisors would like; they will be reluctant to take risks and they will not speak up. Supervisors, in their professional roles, certainly have their own experiences with respect and safety and are in a position to identify with paraprofessionals.

Paraprofessionals are keenly aware of both concepts. Two years ago we conducted a session with all paraprofessionals of a human service agency and asked them to identify what they needed from their supervisors. They were assured that their supervisors would see only their responses, but not their names. "Do you think this will make any real difference?" they asked. They were assured that the supervisors would use this feedback to develop better strategies for training and development. The following sample of the paraprofessionals' responses is reflective of the total response. The question again was, "What do you need from your supervisors?"

- Understanding and recognition.
- Feedback: How am I doing?
- Empathy: Put yourself in my shoes.
- More time and support.
- More open discussion about complaints.
- More equal treatment, no favorites.
- More personal interest in us.
- We need you to listen to our problems.
- I need you to be on my side.
- We need you to speak up for us.
- I need you to talk to me as an adult.
- We need you to meet with us more often.
- We need you to understand without criticizing.
- I need you to understand when I make a mistake.
- Less micromanaging of everything we do.
- Listen if I say it won't work.
- Make us feel important.
- Let others know what we've done.
- Understand that sometimes it just doesn't work.
- Empower us; don't hold us back; encourage us.
- More recognition for working under the adverse conditions we encounter every day.
- Realize that I am intelligent and don't need to be so closely supervised.

- Realize I have another life!
- I need you to trust me.
- Show concern for the problems we have with some coworkers.
- Discuss any criticism of me directly with me and not in a group.
- Understand I don't catch on as quickly as some others. (S. Baker, personal communication, November 3, 1995).

Upon seeing these comments, the supervisors were somewhat taken aback. They said, "I already do these things!" or "Oh, I know who wrote this one!" However, after they examined their own needs for respect and safety, the supervisors offered strategies for building better respect and safety with the paraprofessionals:

- Let them know I have made mistakes in the past . . . it's okay to make mistakes because we learn from what hurts us.
- Support them, be their defender. Ask for ideas. Be sure not to shoot down any ideas they may offer.
- Schedule time to regularly share concerns and success as a group.
- Show a genuine interest in them.
- Share ideas, exchange roles, make home visits, give positive feedback.
- Never compare the performance of one paraprofessional with that of another.
- Allow them, whenever possible, to make decisions for themselves.
- Take more time to listen.
- Have more open discussions about problems—from their perspectives as well as mine. (S. Baker, personal communication, November 3, 1995)

It is apparent that both groups wanted more open discussion. Without first carefully establishing an atmosphere of respect and safety, it is unlikely that such open discussions will be successful. Building respect and safety must start immediately—from the moment of the very first interview—and continue through the initial training. Both factors are critical to the transition process for newly hired paraprofessionals.

## SUMMARY

Human service paraprofessionals benefit tremendously from a supported transition period. They want help, they want feedback, and they want their supervisor's time. The transition period should not be left to chance but should be carefully planned and implemented.

# CHAPTER 6

## Ongoing Training

Maximizing paraprofessional potential continues through ongoing training and performance management. It is ill-advised to leave this next level of training to the unpredictable elements of on-the-job training, particularly with new human service paraprofessionals who need structure, repetition, practice, and support. They require ongoing training specifically designed to encourage and challenge while at the same time adding layers of knowledge and new skills to their repertoires.

In this chapter we consider the situations that call for ongoing training and ways to assess the training needs. We then discuss various formats and venues that have proved consistent with the needs of paraprofessionals. Finally, we provide a brief overview of training principles and an example of a formal training session.

## THE SITUATIONS THAT CALL FOR ONGOING TRAINING

We have identified at least six circumstances that call for ongoing training both for newly hired and already employed human service paraprofessionals. They include the need to build upon existing skills; to re-visit difficult tasks; to enhance co-worker relationships; to address changes in subject matter; to adapt to changes in expected program outcomes; and to adjust to changes in organizations.

## Building Upon Current Skill and Knowledge Levels

However good the initial training program is, it cannot possibly provide new paraprofessionals with everything they will need to function at levels above minimum expectations. It is the supervisor's responsibility to continually provide training that allows them to grow and exceed standards. Although this responsibility may appear obvious, paraprofessionals are often left to their own resources and on-the-job training after the initial training has been completed. In fact, the training never stops, and neither does the supervisor's role in it.

## Revisiting Difficult Tasks

Each new paraprofessional will perform some tasks with relative ease and others with great difficulty. Therefore, it may be necessary to provide training that revisits difficult tasks. Examples of such tasks include recruiting new program participants, interviewing clients, handling difficult clients, accurately completing required paper work, and taking clients through an entire program. From one individual to the next, certain subject matters may prove more difficult than others, from one individual to the next. New paraprofessionals, particularly, need the time and support of their supervisors as well as additional training to overcome these hurdles.

## Managing Coworker Relationships

A third situation that requires ongoing training is when a supervisor observes paraprofessionals having difficulties managing coworker relationships. Handling a multitask position is difficult enough for new human service paraprofessionals. At the same time, they are confronted with the need to form and maintain good relationships with coworkers, most of whom were not part of their initial training and, therefore, not part of their original group. Ongoing training may be required to smooth the transitions and to teach better communication skills.

## Handling Subject Matter Changes

In some instances subject matter changes. A few years ago the United States Department of Agriculture (USDA) ceased referring to the "Four Food Groups" and began designing nutrition education by using the new "Food Guide Pyramid." Educators at all levels immediately had to be trained in the use of this new concept. This retraining included, among others, thousands of paraprofessional nutrition educators. Subject matter changes are common in these days of high technology and rapid research. Examples include changes in nutrition requirements for pregnant women, changes in safety procedures for young children in car seats, and changes in drug-prevention strategies.

## Adapting to Changes in Program-Outcome Expectations

Another change that has ongoing training implications is a change in expected program outcomes. A public agency may be directed to improve certain outcomes, such as infant mortality rates or rates of immunization. A foster care program may be notified that it must increase the number of eventual adoptions or reunited families from the current level to a higher one. A social service agency may be instructed to increase its rate of moving families off support payments. Each of these situations is likely to require additional staff training, even for the most competent employees.

## Adjusting to Organizational Changes

Sometimes programs are completely restructured, either through internal procedures or external mandate. Recent reforms have brought major changes to large public agencies that employ paraprofessionals (such as departments of social services and public health departments). Supervisors in these organizations must provide training for paraprofessionals that will allow them to meet new requirements.

Most human service agencies collaborate with other agencies (for example, public health with Cooperative Extension). Even though one's own agency may not have changed, other agencies with which it collaborates may have changed in ways that will require retraining for paraprofessionals so they can work with their newly restructured partners. Changes in county and state governments may also force change and retraining upon paraprofessionals. Regardless of the situation that calls for training, supervisors must commit themselves to the ongoing training needs of paraprofessionals.

## ASSESSING THE TRAINING NEEDS

Supervisors may become aware of training needs that are not necessarily organizational or subject matter in nature, by systematically observing paraprofessionals on the job. Observation affords a baseline by which past (and future) actions may be compared and contrasted to determine how adequate the training has been. Observation gives the paraprofessionals— especially the new ones—a good sense of the supervisor's genuine interest and confidence in them.

Nearly all human service paraprofessionals work closely with other agencies. In many cases, developing relationships with other agencies is part of the job description. Supervisors may request that the appropriate personnel from these agencies provide feedback on the performance of paraprofessionals. This feedback may cast new light upon training needs that otherwise might go unnoticed.

Paraprofessionals themselves may be asked direct, open-ended questions about their on-the-job experiences, questions such as: "Tell me about your recruiting efforts" or "What would help you to better accomplish your job?" or "What is going best for you right now?" Feedback that the authors have received from training sessions over the years consistently reveals that paraprofessionals want to be asked how their work is proceeding.

## THE FORMATS AND LOCATIONS
## OF ONGOING TRAINING

Ongoing training may be either situational, that is, responding to particular situations as they arise, or planned, such as a year-long training plan for a particular group. Both situational and planned training can be conducted informally or formally. Informal training is primarily a one-to-one format (although it may also be used for a larger group) and is conducted in a non-classroom environment. It is characterized as being more individualized than the typical formal training. "Informal," however, does not imply that the training is unplanned or haphazard. It is more an issue of the training environment and approach than of planning. Our experience has shown that the informal interactions that take place between supervisors and paraprofessionals provide excellent training opportunities. Skills may be developed, new skills may be added, and problems can be solved in a manner geared to the immediate needs of the paraprofessional.

We recognize at least five training venues, the first four of which relate to the training location: in the supervisor's office; on the job; in a training facility located on-site; and at off-site locations. With today's emphasis on alternative training formats (such as distance learning, correspondence, cable and E-mail classes), our fifth location may be a home or library. The other factor we consider is whether the training is conducted on a one-to-one basis or within the context of a larger group. Either of these possibilities may be planned or situational, at any of the locations, and may be formal or informal.

Our experience confirms the value of informal, one-on-one training with new paraprofessionals who are still becoming accustomed to having so much to learn and to being constantly evaluated. They are making no small adjustment, moving from an initial training period where they were with a known group and had the supervisor's full attention, into a training environment where all employees attend. While they are making these adjustments, supervisors may use informal training opportunities to build relationships, to encourage, renew, review, reiterate, and teach. If supervisors have accomplished the "high relationship" component of the initial training and supported transition, new paraprofessionals should be receptive to learning.

A problem area that many paraprofessionals have, for instance, is managing time. Their skills may be improving, but their output is still too low. The supervisor, at that moment and in the office, asks the paraprofessional to refer to the planning calendar and review activities. The supervisor may ask, "What do you have planned for each hour on Monday? What could you do if one of your clients is not at home? Let's think of all the possibilities. Which ones are really possible? What kind of preparation could you do?" Paraprofessionals can learn to devise alternative plans and to execute these plans with ease. Typically they do not arrive on the job with these skills. The informal training session is immediate and geared to the individual. It is also a continuation of relationship building that is so important to helping paraprofessionals achieve their potential.

Every situation where paraprofessionals are employed will be different and supervisory time will vary accordingly. We do not suggest that every program should have ongoing training across all formats and venues, nor do we suggest that we have exhausted all training possibilities here. We are suggesting that (1) planning for ongoing training is important; (2) consistency and quality are vital; and (3) every effort should be made to use informal training opportunities to build paraprofessional potential.

## OVERVIEW OF TRAINING PRINCIPLES

We propose an overall training approach that is based on posing problems, on getting learners to engage in dialogue and on learners learning-by-doing (Vella, 1994, 1995). The content and concepts should be grounded immediately in the learners' own lives. They should have ample opportunities to share on-the-job experiences, to practice new skills in the training environment and to reflect upon what they have learned and how the learning will be applied. Learning tasks should be problem based so that participants work with the content, generate solutions, give meaning to what they are learning and make the content their own.

The least appropriate training model for paraprofessionals is that which features a lecture or monologue given by the trainer. A common mistake made by trainers is to rely greatly upon lecture, with minor support from printed materials (including overhead transparencies and handouts). Supervisors should observe that effective training is a great deal more than simply telling paraprofessionals what they need to know in order to affect behavioral change among their clients. Adult learners generally prefer learning visually, interactively, and with "hands-on" involvement.

At the very least, training designs for paraprofessionals should reach beyond a Level 2 interaction (referred to earlier in Chapter 4). Training outcomes should improve immediately merely by shifting to higher levels of interaction and by promoting discussion and dialogue among participants. In addition, paraprofessionals are generally eager to share experiences with each other. Ongoing training sessions should include opportunities for this type of sharing, brainstorming, and critiquing.

Another way to ensure more effective training is to utilize Vella's (1994, 1995) seven steps of planning (illustrated in Chapter 4, Figure 4.1). Following the steps requires the supervisor/ trainer to thoroughly consider who the participants are, why this training is being provided, when and where it will be conducted, what will be included, what will be accomplished and how it will be accomplished. The seven-step plan features achievement objectives (the What For? step) which are written with action verbs. Participants practice new skills while they are receiving the training.

Figure 6.1 is an example of a training session designed according to the seven steps of planning. A topic has been selected

| Materials: | VCR/Monitor, 3-minute video clip, Post-It notes, markers. |
| Who: | Eight paraprofessionals who mentor young pregnant women in an urban area. |
| Why: | The paraprofessionals have indicated they are finding it difficult to really listen to their clients because they are distracted by noisy living environments and also thinking ahead to plan what they should say. |
| When: | Tuesday afternoon, 1:00—2:00. |
| Where: | Office training facility. |
| What: | Barriers to listening. Active-listening skills. |
| What For: | By the end of this session, participants 1. Will have critiqued a video clip that depicts a poor-listening situation. 2. Will have generated strategies to improve a poor-listening situation. 3. Will have practiced four active-listening skills. |

| How: | Task # 1: | For a warm-up, participants will list everything they hear for two minutes. They will then share their lists with everyone else. |
| | Task # 2: | Participants will be shown a video clip of a mentoring session depicting a mentor attempting to listen to a client while encountering several barriers. Participants, as they view the video clip, will jot down all the barriers they see. (The video clip may be shown twice, if necessary, since it is only 3 minutes long.) |
| | Task # 3: | Participants will discuss with a partner what might be done to improve the listening situation depicted in the video clip. |
| | Task # 4: | After listening to a brief, 3-minute lecture on four active-listening skills, the participants will write down a concern they have about their work. Each person will then share her concern with another person who will attempt to use the four active-listening skills (paraphrasing, clarifying, questioning, and asking open-ended questions). |
| | Task # 5: | Participants will share with the group at least one listening strategy they want to try right away with their clients. |

**Figure 6.1.** "Listen . . . Do You Want to Know a Secret?" Active-Listening Skills Training.

that is applicable to nearly any working situation, but particularly for human service paraprofessionals. Not all details (such as seating arrangements, charts, and handouts) have been included but are also important to the overall success of the session.

The What For? items (achievement objectives) are always written in terms of "the participants will have . . . " (instead of the traditional "Participants will be able to . . . " or "Participants will have knowledge of . . . "). Achievement-based objectives ensure that participants actually practice new skills and apply concepts while in the training environment. Paraprofessionals may be taught to use the seven steps of planning in their own work and will benefit from seeing them frequently modeled.

## SUMMARY

In conclusion, ongoing training for paraprofessionals should receive the same commitment, time, and planning as every other component of the Sequential Development Model. Informal ongoing training has proved especially effective with paraprofessionals because they benefit greatly from the immediacy of the training and the encouragement of the supervisor. Ongoing training is the element needed to help paraprofessionals improve their skills beyond minimum performance expectations and move toward levels that exceed expectations.

# CHAPTER 7

## Performance Management

Managers, supervisors, and administrators of human service agencies generally agree on their mutual displeasure with the subject of performance appraisal. It is the sort of topic that immediately brings to mind a myriad of negative thoughts, tense emotions, and unpleasant memories. Human service organizations are in the business of helping people, and the supervisors of such organizations generally have backgrounds in the fields of public health, nutrition, social work, and education. Frequently these individuals were attracted to their fields of study and work because they had a desire to help people. They are, by nature, a nonjudgmental group. To them, by contrast, the idea of performance appraisal seems rather judgmental.

Performance appraisal, however, should not be viewed in isolation. Rather, it should be seen as but one element of a comprehensive performance management system. Performance management is the ongoing process which includes performance expectations, ongoing coaching and feedback, midyear appraisals, and the annual appraisal interview.

As described by Maddux (1987), "A performance appraisal provides a periodic opportunity for communication between the person who assigns the work and the person who performs it, to discuss what they expect from the other and how well those expectations are being met" (p. 6). Concerning the appraisal interview, he describes it as "an essential communication link between two people with a common purpose" (p. 6). Good appraisal of performance requires the establishment of an agreement between the parties concerning specific outcomes that should be expected and attained. If these performance standards are not clearly set forth, the evaluation of performance will be an arduous exercise for both parties.

In performance management, it is the supervisor's responsibility to help employees achieve success, instead of prodding them toward better performance. By giving paraprofessionals responsibility for results and then measuring the degree to which results are achieved, a situation is created in which their sense of self-worth is linked with the achievement of organizational objectives. Focusing on the development of the employee while addressing the organization's need for performance accountability is often a comfortable way for human service providers to accomplish their task of employee appraisal.

This chapter begins with a discussion of the roles and responsibilities of the supervisor pertaining to performance management. Next, preparation of both paraprofessionals and supervisors for the appraisal interview is discussed. Specific strategies for actually conducting the performance appraisal interview are then presented. Since supervisors sometimes inherit ongoing programs and the responsibility for performance appraisal, strategies are offered that may make this difficult situation more manageable and positive. Finally, linking training to performance goals is offered as a strategy for planning ongoing training.

## ROLES AND RESPONSIBILITIES
## OF THE SUPERVISOR

The supervisor's role in performance management begins with employees before they are hired. Prospective employees should understand clearly the performance standards by which they will be evaluated. Soon after beginning a new job, employees should be instructed about the performance management system currently used by the organization. The supervisor should provide a copy of the performance appraisal instrument designed for their specific position, review it with the employees, and then explain the performance appraisal interview process to them.

Additionally, the supervisor should consider sharing specific, measurable performance standards with each employee. "Performance standards have two purposes: They give employees a guide to behavior needed to accomplish their jobs' results and they provide a basis against which an individual's performance can be fairly appraised" (ASTD, 1990, p. 3). By sharing these performance standards immediately after paraprofessionals are hired, the supervisor is setting the stage for relationships with them. The supervisor is expressing concern for each employee's success by clearly identifying expectations.

## Informal Coaching and Feedback

We discussed the importance of coaching and feedback earlier, in Chapter 5. Both of these supervisory roles are components of the overall performance management system. Employees deserve regular feedback from their supervisors. Most people think of the annual performance appraisal as the formal feedback given in writing. However, unplanned informal feedback, as an immediate response to a specific behavior, is generally valued even more by employees. Similarly, coaching is most effective when it occurs spontaneously as a result of informal interactions between the employee and the supervisor.

The supervisor is responsible for ensuring that regular opportunities for coaching and feedback occur. How is this accomplished? Certainly the supervisor must be accessible to employees. Accessibility, however, is substantially more than merely leaving the office door open. Supervisors should communicate their schedules to their staffs. Also, they should take steps to approach their subordinates, that is, employees should not have to constantly seek out their supervisor. When asked what attribute was desirable in a supervisor, a paraprofessional answered, "She should be there when I need her" (C. Meekins, personal communication, November 4, 1996). These informal, individual exchanges with an employee may be regarded as opportunities for development. While addressing issues that may be unique to that employee the supervisor is cementing the supervisor-employee relationship.

## Formal Feedback

In addition to the critical informal opportunities for coaching and feedback, the supervisor is responsible for scheduling regular, formal meetings—conferences—with each employee. With most professionals, these conferences may be scheduled quarterly or semiannually. Paraprofessionals, in contrast, benefit from formal feedback on a monthly basis. Supervisors may respond that they do not have sufficient time to meet monthly with every paraprofessional. An hour per month spent with each paraprofessional, however, can dramatically increase efficiency and effectiveness.

At quarterly intervals the supervisor should meet with employees individually to discuss their performance and how it compares to established performance standards, as well as progress made toward specific goals. This time is also appropriate for reviewing the performance appraisal instrument and the appraisal interview process.

To keep this process streamlined and organized, supervisors may establish a file for each employee. This file will be a convenient place for maintaining records related to each employee. For example, supervisors might include in this file (1) notes from conferences with the employee; (2) issues that need follow-up action; (3) correspondence relating to the employee; (4) notes from observations of the employee's performance throughout the year; and (5) statistics relative to performance.

## Challenge and Support

Supervisors should provide opportunities that challenge paraprofessionals to reach outside their performance comfort zones. At the same time, supervisors provide the support that paraprofessionals need as they take these risks. The appropriate combination of formal and informal opportunities for coaching and feedback will provide paraprofessionals with the courage and confidence to take risks and ultimately exceed expectations. When paraprofessionals are given individualized and specific expectations, they generally achieve them. However, paraprofessionals who are not challenged with specific expectations, as a rule, do not achieve the same level of performance.

## Observation of Performance

Regular opportunities to observe each paraprofessional's performance should be scheduled by the supervisor. These observations should be scheduled on a quarterly basis, more often for new employees, or if performance problems are apparent. A checklist or observation form will help supervisors gather information across consistent categories. It will also allow the supervisor to occasionally ask other individuals to observe. Of course, paraprofessionals should receive feedback after their performance is observed.

## PREPARING PARAPROFESSIONALS FOR THE APPRAISAL INTERVIEW

Paraprofessionals should be encouraged to prepare for the performance appraisal interview and be made aware of all topics that will be addressed. With appropriate planning by the paraprofessional and the supervisor, the appraisal interview will be a productive dialogue. The specific time for the appraisal interview should be agreeable to both parties and fixed in advance (Maddux, 1987). One approach is to provide paraprofessionals with a copy of the appraisal form and ask them to rate their performance prior to the appraisal interview. This exercise will help them prepare to address the topics during the interview. In addition, the supervisor may suggest additional questions to think about before the appraisal interview takes place. Examples of questions include the following:

- What do I like best about my job? What do I like least?
- How could my supervisor help me do a better job?
- Does the organization or my supervisor do anything that hinders my performance?
- What changes would improve my performance?

A certain amount of anxiety and concern typically characterizes performance appraisal interviews. However, if supervisors discuss performance with paraprofessionals throughout the year, the level of anxiety can be reduced (ASTD, May 1990). In other words, the appraisal interview is no time for surprises! Paraprofessionals should experience the appraisal as a culmination of multiple, informal conversations that have taken place throughout the year.

## PREPARATION REQUIREMENTS
## FOR SUPERVISORS

Performance appraisal is defined as "the identification, evaluation, and development of individual performance" (ASTD, May 1990, p. 1). Evaluations should be based on a combination of objective observations and accomplishments as compared to specific job standards. The appraisal interview should address performance issues rather than personality. Comparisons are made between the employee's actual performance and the expected performance outlined in job standards.

Clearly, effective performance appraisal interviews require preparation by the supervisor. The supervisor will want to (1) review organizational policies and procedures relating to appraisals; (2) consult previous appraisals to identify strengths, weaknesses, goals, and plans for performance improvement; (3) review program records that relate to quality and quantity of work and documentation from observations of performance; (4) review all records relating to the paraprofessional's performance and notes made throughout the year; and (5) complete the appraisal form and identify topics for discussion during the interview as well as potential goals for improvement of performance.

Maddux (1987) identifies four fundamental areas that should be addressed in a performance appraisal interview:

1. The measurement of the results of the employee's performance against goals and/or standards.

2. Recognition of the employee's contributions.

3. Correction of any new or ongoing performance problems.

4. The establishment of goals and or standards for the next appraisal period (p. 30)

## CONDUCTING THE PERFORMANCE APPRAISAL INTERVIEW

The tone of the interview should be set by the supervisor. The interview should begin in a manner that encourages the paraprofessional to participate in a dialogue, rather than listen to the supervisor speak for the entire time. The interview should be a "job-related discussion that confirms employees' understanding of their job duties" (ASTD, May 1990, p. 6). Sharing the agenda with the employee may help to set all parties at ease.

### Steps for Conducting Appraisal Interviews

Job standards should be addressed one by one, first by the paraprofessional who offers a self-assessment, and then by the supervisor. (Supervisors should be prepared to share documentation of this assessment, in the form of reports, and notes from observations.) The supervisors may listen and respond to the paraprofessional's comments without necessarily agreeing. Feedback should be offered in a positive manner with emphasis on those aspects of performance that are favorably regarded. Paraprofessionals should be asked to list three strengths. It is important for the supervisor to compliment the paraprofessional on any above-average performances and accomplishments, including job-related skills, competencies or interpersonal skills. Specific suggestions should be offered for any below standard areas. Sufficient time should be allowed so that the paraprofessional is afforded the opportunity to comprehend the evaluation process.

Paraprofessionals should be asked to share the areas that they identified for improvement. The supervisor may suggest additional ones and discuss techniques for achieving results. In addition, the supervisor should work with the employee to identify how the supervisor might specifically assist the paraprofessional in making improvements.

Goals identified by both parties should be examined and compared. Consensus may then be reached on which goals should be recorded on the appraisal instrument. These goals should be listed specifically, generally including areas where the paraprofessional may seek to strengthen specific skills or attempt a new skill or technique. The supervisor may refer to the areas identified for improvement and link them to future goals when possible.

It is the supervisor's responsibility to bring closure to the interview. Generally, closure includes summarizing the discussion, listing any plans agreed upon for improvement, and reiterating the performance expectations associated with the position. The paraprofessional's signature should be secured and the interview closed with comments of thanks from the supervisor. The original form will be sent to the human resources office (or to the appropriate department) for inclusion in the paraprofessional's personnel file. The supervisor retains a copy and provides one for the paraprofessional.

## WHAT IF YOU INHERIT AN
## ONGOING PROGRAM?

Supervisors often find themselves having to evaluate the performance of paraprofessionals soon after assuming a supervisory position. They may have had insufficient time on the job to adequately observe the performance of the paraprofessionals. Actually, the supervisors may still be learning what the job standards are! In such situations, we offer this advice: Supervisors should pass the buck if at all possible. Perhaps an administrator will be available who may be prevailed upon to conduct the interview during the interim period. If no one else is available or willing to assist, the new supervisor should research the performance standards, previous appraisal instruments, and any records relevant to performance. Another strategy for the new supervisor is to seek the advice and counsel of other supervisors in similar capacities.

## Share the Limitations

During the appraisal interview it is best for the new supervisor to share in a forthright manner his or her limitations about the situation. The supervisor can refer to last year's appraisal form and ask for the paraprofessional's input about improvements, strengths, and weaknesses. By addressing this less-than-ideal situation honestly, the supervisor may well gain the respect of the paraprofessional.

## Clarify the Expectations

New supervisors generally do not have access to the specific expectations that were shared previously with individual paraprofessionals. This interview, then, represents an important opportunity for the new supervisor to clarify performance expectations and to explain the new method by which performance will be evaluated. The clarification of expectations will eliminate any confusion that the paraprofessional may have and will provide the appropriate groundwork for future discussions related to performance. This discussion will also help the supervisor and paraprofessional develop their working relationship.

Supervisors should look upon these discussions as investments that will pay dividends over the long term.

## LINKING TRAINING TO PERFORMANCE GOALS

Supervisors are responsible for determining training needs and designing training programs to address these needs. If performance management is taken seriously and is well executed, it will provide the training needs-assessment information that is required to accurately determine the needs of the paraprofessionals. Information gained through this ongoing performance management process relative to performance deficits becomes the basis for training programs.

A strong performance management system is especially important when working with human service paraprofessionals. Our experience has been that they want feedback, they want more time with supervisors, and they want to improve their performance. Additionally, paraprofessionals want to be assured that what they do really makes a difference. When paraprofessionals ask, "How am I doing?" their interest is not only in themselves but in how they compare to others and how their actions make a difference to the entire program. Supervisors should employ strategies that allow paraprofessionals to see their performance as part of a team and as part of the total program.

If supervisors are successful at positioning performance appraisals as just one part of a comprehensive performance management system, the appraisal interview will not be an isolated and dreaded incident. Rather, it will serve as an opportunity to celebrate performance, identify strengths and weaknesses, and set goals for the future. The authors have experienced positive, empowering, and motivating performance appraisal interviews with underachieving paraprofessionals. The paraprofessionals were making progress and could see that progress documented, and they were well prepared for this component of the performance management system.

# CHAPTER 8

## Further Reflections on Maximizing Paraprofessional Potential

In this final chapter we briefly examine some issues that relate to the use and training of paraprofessionals and offer them for further consideration. These issues should be of interest, not only to direct supervisors, but also to administrators who make program decisions. In our discussion of one issue—time—we include strategies that should help supervisors achieve immediate improvements in their staff training and program outcomes even if they are unable to implement the entire Sequential Development Model.

### ISSUES

Olson (1994) looked specifically for research that addressed the impact of training on paraprofessionals. Most of the studies she found, however, focused on client outcomes and not training outcomes for paraprofessionals themselves. *How can paraprofessional training be evaluated?* Are the training processes appropriate? Does the training actually close performance gaps? Have behaviors changed? Has the organization improved? A well-designed system of evaluating training in terms of outcomes (both during the after training) would give supervisors constant feedback on how well they are doing. As Olson found, at least with nutrition programs, such evaluation systems rarely existed.

*What responsibility do supervisors have to help their paraprofessionals eventually leave their position and advance to more responsible roles or to additional education?* We believe in planning and designing for the growth and development of the paraprofessional. Thus, career development is built in because skills are being developed, more complex strategies are being implemented and more difficult problems are being solved.

If the paraprofessional position is treated as an opportunity for growth and development, *how can that growth be measured?* What practices are most likely to result in growth? Ideally, supervisors should have more than anecdotal evidence to guide them in their training practices. If growth occurs along a continuum, for instance, between concrete and abstract, how can that growth be assessed?

It is tempting to select an applicant for a paraprofessional position who already has a college degree and subject-matter knowledge. *What are the outcomes when professionals are hired for human service paraprofessional positions?* Will the professional fit comfortably into a paraprofessional position with co-workers who do not have similar educational backgrounds or future aspirations? How long will the degreed person remain in the position? Does it matter? Does any research exist that actually compares and contrasts program outcomes between professionals and paraprofessionals working in the same setting?

*When paraprofessionals are hired to teach, will they be taught how to teach, or will they be given a prescribed curriculum or script and asked not to stray from it?* Human service paraprofessionals are usually selected on the basis of their forecasted ability to relate to clients on a more personal level because their life experiences and backgrounds are similar to the clients. How is that common background a benefit when their actions are strictly prescribed?

## TIME

As noted on several occasions throughout this volume, maximizing paraprofessional potential requires time. We also realize that many supervisors, at least for the moment, may not have the amount of time we envision. One of the strengths of the Sequential Development Model is that it can be implemented in increments, with each implementation by itself having a potentially great impact on paraprofessional training and program outcomes.

Program outcomes can be improved immediately if, before the hiring process begins, supervisors take the time to determine (1) exactly what the paraprofessionals will be asked to do; and (2) what basic work skills applicants should be expected to bring to the job. Having this knowledge in advance allows supervisors to design appropriate interview questions and make sound hiring decisions.

Supervisors may begin viewing informal encounters with paraprofessionals as excellent training opportunities. As noted in Chapter 6, informal training for paraprofessionals can be a very effective means of improving their skills and performance in an immediate and highly relevant way. In addition, supervisors can improve all training immediately by designing for at least Level Three interactions, also discussed in Chapter 6.

Finally, performance management can be improved by making the performance evaluation instrument a familiar, useful, and nonintimidating tool for paraprofessionals.

These strategies are practical for all supervisors of paraprofessionals, even those who are unable to devote the amount of time they would like to training. As programs continue, supervisors may implement additional practices that will improve both the skills of the paraprofessionals and the program outcomes.

## SUMMARY

Properly trained paraprofessionals have great potential to act in meaningful and measurable ways as agents of change in the lives of their clients, assisting them in improving the quality of their lives. Human service paraprofessionals can have a unique and positive impact on some of the problems faced by our society: not only do they provide much-needed services, but they also serve as excellent role models. At the same time, paraprofessionals themselves, when given the opportunity, are able to attain levels of skill that they may have previously thought unimaginable, functioning as more than mere extensions of professionals. As trainers and supervisors of paraprofessional employees, we can do significantly more than hire them and send them out with someone who "knows the ropes."

The Sequential Development Model for Maximizing Paraprofessional Potential provides a strong foundation and blueprint for supervisors who want to build their paraprofessionals' skills and help them achieve excellent program results. Outstanding, tangible effects may confidently be anticipated by (1) analyzing the job and its tasks; (2) basing the selection of paraprofessionals on the results of the job/task analysis; (3) providing solid initial training that is tied to the competencies measured by the performance appraisal process; (4) providing a period of supported transition; (5) conducting immediate and relevant ongoing training; and (6) continually tying performance management and the appraisal process into all training efforts.

# APPENDIX A

A Performance
Appraisal Instrument

**North Carolina**
**Cooperative Extension Service**

NORTH CAROLINA STATE UNIVERSITY
COLLEGE OF AGRICULTURE & LIFE SCIENCES

**EXPANDED FOOD AND NUTRITION EDUCATION PROGRAM**
**EXTENSION NUTRITION PROGRAM ASSISTANT**
**ANNUAL EVALUATION OF PERFORMANCE**

Adult Nutrition Program Assistant _____

County _____

Date _____

## ADULT EFNEP PERFORMANCE STANDARDS

Nutrition Program Assistant workload is the total number of teaching contacts completed with eligible homemakers per month.

### Workload Minimum

Program Assistant should complete at least 66 teaching contacts with enrolled homemakers in a typical month (one without leave), working 30 hours per week. (Minimum = 66)

### Workload Targets

**Rural** 70–75 teaching contacts per month, & formation of at least two groups.

**Urban** 75–85 contacts per month, & Formation of at least five groups.

| OVERALL RATING | Points |
|---|---|
| 5 { } Excellent | 100–90 |
| 4 { } Commendable | 89–80 |
| 3 { } Satisfactory | 79–65 |
| 2 { } Conditional | 64–55 |
| 1 { } Unacceptable | 54–Below |

**Signatures and dates:**
Nutrition Program Assistant: _____ Date

(My signature does not necessarily indicate concurrence)
Supervising Agent _____ Date

County Extension Director _____ Date

CIRCLE THE APPROPRIATE NUMBER IN EACH CATEGORY

| 1. QUANTITY OF WORK | EXCELLENT | GOOD | FAIR | POOR | COMMENTS |
|---|---|---|---|---|---|
| WORKLOAD *(See recommended work-loads on Page 1) | Exceeds recommended number of teaching contacts per month. **14** | Meets recommended number of teaching contacts per month. **12** | Meets minimum number of teaching contacts per month. **5** | Meets *less* than minimum number of teaching contacts per month. **0** | |
| GROUPS *(See recommended group levels on Page 1) | Exceeds recommended minimum number of groups. **10** | Meets recommended minimum number of groups. **8** | Meets less than minimum number of groups. **3** | Makes little or no effort to teach in groups. **0** | |
| TARGET AUDIENCE | 100% of homemakers have incomes at or below the poverty level & have children in the home/pregnant. **3** | 90% of families are at or below poverty level & have children in the home/pregnant. **2** | | 10% or more of homemakers are over-income or do not have children in the home/pregnant. **0** | |
| RECRUITING FAMILIES | Successfully maintains a minimum of 20 enrolled homemakers/with on-going recruiting. **5** | Is successful when recruiting homemakers but does not recruit as often as necessary to maintain case load. **3** | Spends much time recruiting with little results. **2** | Makes little effort and is not effective in recruiting homemakers into the program. **0** | |

109

| 1. QUANTITY OF WORK | EXCELLENT | GOOD | FAIR | POOR | COMMENTS |
|---|---|---|---|---|---|
| AFFIRMATIVE ACTION | Racial balance of annual case load is approximately the ratio of low-income families (black/white & other races) in the assigned area. **4** | Case load is integrated. **3** | Continuously attempts to integrate case load. **2** | Little or no attempt is made to integrate the case load. **0** | |

| 2. QUALITY OF WORK | EXCELLENT | GOOD | FAIR | POOR | COMMENTS |
|---|---|---|---|---|---|
| KNOWLEDGE OF FOOD AND NUTRITION | Demonstrates better than adequate understanding of subject matter & gives accurate information. **6** | Demonstrates adequate understanding of subject matter; and gives accurate information. **5** | Demonstrates a limited understanding of subject matter; most information given is accurate. **2** | Does not know subject matter. Gives out some inaccurate information. **0** | |
| MEETING HOMEMAKERS' NEEDS | Consistently bases teaching plans for each homemaker or group on needs identified from family record, food recalls & "EFNEP Survey" assessment. **5** | Makes some effort to base teaching plans on needs identified from family record, food recalls & "EFNEP Survey" assessment. **4** | Bases teaching plans on existing materials rather than needs identified. **2** | Does not make teaching plans for homemakers in advance. **0** | |

| | Excellent Quality of Work. 6 | Acceptable Quality of Work 5 | | Unacceptable/ Needs improvement. 0 |
|---|---|---|---|---|
| TEACHING TECHNIQUES **As documented in "Observation of Teaching Visit in EFNEP" forms (Average rating, from 3 or 4 observations per year). | | | | |
| RESULTS OF TEACHING | 85–100% of the families are improving diets and scores on "EFNEP Survey" assessment. 6 | 70–85% of the families are improving diets and scores on "EFNEP Survey" assessment. 5 | 50–70% of the families are improving diets and scores on "EFNEP Survey" assessment. 2 | Less than half of the families are improving diets & scores on "EFNEP Survey" assessment. 0 |
| PROGRESSION OF HOME-MAKERS | Moves 90% of families through the program within 6 months 6 | Moves at least 75% of families through the program within 6 months 4 | Moves at least 60% of families through the program within 6 months 2 | Moves fewer than 60% of families through the program within 6 months 0 |

| 3A. WORK HABITS | EXCELLENT | GOOD | FAIR | POOR | COMMENTS |
|---|---|---|---|---|---|
| ATTENDANCE & PUNCTUALITY | Never late or absent without notice. 3 | Seldom late or absent without notice. 2 | Frequently late or absent without notice. -3 | Habitually late or absent without notice. -10 | |
| PLANNING FOR VISITS | Prepares weekly work schedule and keeps supervisor informed of substantial changes. 4 | Prepares weekly work schedule, but may not follow or notify supervisor of changes. 3 | Seldom follows weekly work schedule. 1 | Does not follow a weekly work schedule. 0 | |
| USE OF TIME | Schedules visits in advance. Averages 3–6 teaching visits/6 hour day. Exceeds minimum number of teaching contacts. 6 | Schedules visits in advance. Averages minimum teaching contacts per 6 hour day. 5 | Schedule visits in advance. Makes fewer than minimum teaching contacts per 6 hour day. 2 | Teaching visits not scheduled in advance. 1 | |
| RECORDS AND REPORTS | Records always on time, accurate, and up to date. 4 | Records on time— usually accurate and complete. 3 | Records are often late or inaccurate. 1 | Records not kept up to date and are usually late. 0 | |

| 3B. WORK ATTITUDES | EXCELLENT | GOOD | FAIR | POOR | COMMENTS |
|---|---|---|---|---|---|
| IMPROVEMENT OF JOB PER-FORMANCE | Takes initiative in improving job performance. This may include formation of groups, agency cooperation, and/or development. **3** | With minimum direction of supervising agent, makes plans for improvement & meets goals. **2** | With substantial direction of supervising agent, makes plans for improvement & meets goals. **1** | Fails to improve. **0** | |
| VOLUNTEER RECRUITMENT | Recruits and communicates with volunteers. **2** | Makes an effort to recruit volunteers. **1** | | Does not attempt to recruit volunteers. **0** | |

## 3C. RELATIONS WITH OTHERS—OTHER PROGRAM ASSISTANTS, SUPERVISORS, COUNTY EXTENSION STAFF

| | | | | |
|---|---|---|---|---|
| COOPERATION | Receptive to supervision suggestions and constructive criticism. Actively promotes effective relationships with total staff. **4** | Receptive to supervision suggestions and constructive criticism. Usually cooperative with total staff. **3** | Sometimes receptive to supervision, suggestions & constructive criticism. **2** | Uncooperative. **−10** |
| REFERRALS | Knows community resources; makes referrals to appropriate agencies, follows up on referrals, as practical; consults with supervisor as necessary. **3** | Knows most community resources; usually follows up on referrals. **2** | Knows few community resources and makes few attempts to refer families or to follow up on referrals. **1** | Does not follow up on referrals. **0** |
| RAPPORT WITH HOMEMAKERS | Has good teaching relationship with homemakers; shows empathy & respect. **2** | Has good teaching relationship with most homemakers. **1** | | Does not have good teaching relationship with homemakers. **0** |
| CONFIDENTIALITY | Keeps records and information confidential. **4** | | | Discusses EFNEP participants outside EFNEP staff. **−10** |

Number of homemakers worked with during 12 months ending March 31: _____
Average workload_____ .

Graduated: _____
Terminated: _____
# Volunteers: _____
# Groups: _____

# PERFORMANCE REVIEW SUMMARY

A. Progress toward meeting last year's goals.

B. Areas needing improvement.

C. Overall strengths. (List 2 or 3)

D. Goals for strengthening job performance.
Supervising Agent and Nutrition PA together identify 2 or 3 goals to be worked toward in the coming year. Progress to be reviewed during next annual performance evaluation.

Adapted for use in North Carolina from "Annual Evaluation of Extension Aide," University of Maryland.

February 1997

115

# APPENDIX B

## A 4-Week Training Program
(Baker, 1994)

Unit I—Content Outline

Module 1:   Orientation to Organization/Job (3 hours)
A.  Employee benefits
B.  Pretest
C.  EFNEP questionnaire
D.  Extension's mission, vision and goals

Module 2:   EFNEP Roles and Extension Relationships (3 hours)
A.  History of Extension/land-grand institutions
B.  Administrative chain-of-command
C.  Subject matter specialists
D.  History of EFNEP
E.  Program assistants' role in county staff
F.  *The Mission of the EFNEP Program Assistant* (video)

Module 3:   Introduction to *Eating Right Is Basic 2* (2 hours)
A.  Participants receive curriculum
B.  Determining client eligibility
C.  Client enrollment procedures

Module 4:   Making Meals from What's on Hand (3 hours)
A.  Meal planning
B.  Food selection
C.  Food preparation

Module 5:   Nutrients We Need (3 hours)
A.  Introduction to nutrition
B.  *How Food Affects Us* (slide/tape)
C.  *Nutrition in the Life Cycle* (video)
D.  Food preparation

Module 6:   Planning Makes a Difference (3 hours)
A.  Meal planning as part of a healthy diet
B.  Meal planning
C.  Food selection
D.  Food storage
E.  Food preparation

Module 7:   Shopping Basics (3 hours)
A.  Meal planning
B.  Food selection
C.  Food storage
D.  Food preparation

Module 8:   Let's Make Something Simple (2 hours, 30 minutes)
     A.  Meal planning
     B.  Food selection
     C.  Food preparation

Module 9:   Observation/Practice Enrolling With Experienced NPA
     (6 hours)
     A.  Complete *Observation of Teaching Visit* forms
     B.  Look for
       1.  Teaching techniques
       2.  Recruitment techniques
       3.  NPA relationship with participants

Unit II—Content Outline

Module 10:  Progressing EFNEP Audiences (2 hours, 30 minutes)
     A.  *Recruiting Program Families* (video)
     B.  Icebreakers for group instruction
     C.  *Helping People Change* (video)
     D.  *Helping People Learn To Do* (video)

Module 11:  Fruits (4 hours)
     A.  Fruits as part of a healthy diet
     B.  Meal planning
     C.  Food selection
     D.  Food buying
     E.  Food storage
     F.  Food preparation

Module 12:  Referrals—Part 1 (6 hours)
     A.  What is a referral?
     B.  Why make referrals?
     C.  Making appropriate referrals
     D.  Community resources
     E.  Visits to referral agencies
       1.  Food stamps
       2.  AFDC (Aid to Families with Dependent Children)
       3.  Food Bank
       4.  Food Pantry

Module 13:  Referrals—Part 2 (2 hours, 30 minutes)
     A.  Visits to referral agencies
       1.  Local health department

      2.  WIC Supplemental Nutrition Program For Women, Infants and Children

Module 14:  Vegetables (3 hours, 30 minutes)
     A.  Vegetables as part of a healthy diet
     B.  Meal planning
     C.  Food selection
     D.  Food buying
     E.  Food storage
     F.  Food preparation

Module 15:  Milk and Cheese (4 hours)
     A.  Milk and cheese as part of a healthy diet
     B.  Meal planning
     C.  Food selection
     D.  Food buying
     E.  Food storage
     F.  Food preparation

Module 16:  Breads, Cereal, and Pasta (3 hours, 30 minutes)
     A.  Breads, cereal, and pasta as part of a healthy diet
     B.  Meal planning
     C.  Food selection
     D.  Food buying
     E.  Food storage
     F.  Food preparation

Module 17:  Observation/Practice Enrolling with Experienced NPA (6 hours)
     A.  Complete *Observation of Teaching Visit* forms
     B.  Look for
        1.  Teaching techniques
        2.  Recruitment techniques
        3.  NPA relationship with participants

Unit III—Content Outline

Module 18:  Dried Beans and Peas
     A.  Dried beans and peas as part of a healthy diet
     B.  Meal planning
     C.  Food selection
     D.  Food buying
     E.  Food storage
     F.  Food preparation

Module 19: EFNEP Records
    A. Introduction
    B. Why so many records?
    C. Confidentiality of records
    D. Family Record
    E. Dietary Recall
    F. Teaching Record
    G. Enrolling participants
    H. Closure

Module 20: EFNEP Reports
    A. Introduction
    B. Time and Travel Report
    C. County Input and Participation System (CIPS) Report
    D. NPA's List of Families
    E. Weekly Schedule/Program Planning Sheet
    F. Volunteer Report
    G. Closure

Module 21: Work Habits (2 hours)
    A. Attendance and Punctuality
    B. Planning for teaching visits
        1. Weekly schedules
        2. Program planning sheet
    C. Records and reports
    D. Working smarter
    E. Use of time
    F. Using a calendar effectively
        1. Recording contact
        2. Scheduling visits
        3. Mileage
        4. Note for office hours

Module 22: How Adults Learn (2 hours)
    A. Androgogy vs. pedagogy
    B. Principles of learning
    C. Hierarchy of human needs
    D. Factors that influence learning

Module 23: Meat, Poultry, Fish, and Eggs (4 hours)
    A. Principles of normal nutrition
    B. Meal planning
    C. Food selection

      D. Food buying
      E. Food storage
      F. Food preparation

Module 24: Putting It All Together (3 hours)
      A. Principles of normal nutrition
      B. Meal planning
      C. Food selection
      D. Food buying
      E. Food storage
      F. Food preparation
      G. Alternative teaching methods

Module 25: Eating Right for Two (3 hours)
      A. Principles of normal nutrition
      B. Special nutrient needs during pregnancy
      C. Fetal development and weight gain
      D. Things to avoid during pregnancy
      E. Common discomforts during pregnancy
      F. Food preparation

Module 26: Feeding Your Infant (1 hour)
      A. Breastfeeding
      B. Bottle-feeding
      C. Storage of breast milk and formula
      D. Food preparation

Module 27: Feeding Baby Solid Food (1 and 1/2 hours)
      A. Making baby food at home
      B. Comparing baby foods (Food Selection)
      C. Principles of normal nutrition
      D. Food buying
      E. Food storage
      F. Food preparation

Module 28: Observation/Practice Teaching with Experienced NPA (6 hours)
      A. Complete Observation of Teaching Visit Forms
      B. Look for
         1. Teaching techniques
         2. Recruitment techniques
         3. NPA relationship with participants
         4. Time management skills

## Unit IV—Content Outline

Module 29: Feeding Your Preschool Child (3 hours)
    A. Nutritional needs of preschoolers
    B. What makes a good snack?
    C. Feeding tips for preschoolers
    D. How much is a serving?
    E. Food preparation

Module 30: Quantity of Work (2 hours, 30 minutes)
    A. Workload standards and expectations
    B. Group instruction
    C. Recruitment
    D. Affirmative action
    E. Performance evaluation instrument/performance expectations

Module 31: Relations with Others (2 hours, 30 minutes)
    A. Cooperation with coworkers, supervisor
    B. Teamwork
    C. Building relationships or reacting to conflict
    D. Rapport with clients
    E. Volunteer recruitment

Module 32: Target Audience (3 hours, 30 minutes)
    A. Cultural diversity
    B. Differing values, similar needs
    C. Cultural food habits
    D. Why do we eat the things we do?
    E. Cultural food tasting

Module 33: Food Preservation (4 hours)
    A. Bacterial, food-borne illness
    B. Boiling-water-bath canning
    C. Pressure canning
    D. Freezing fruits and vegetables
    E. Drying fruits and vegetables

Module 34: Gardening Basics (2 hours)
    A. Plant your garden on paper first
    B. Container gardening
    C. Gardening tools
    D. Preparing the soil
    E. Planting

F.  Nutrient needs of vegetable garden
G.  Weed control
H.  Harvesting the vegetables

Module 35: Quality of Work (2 hours)
A.  Teaching techniques
B.  Measuring teaching outcomes
C.  Progression of clients
D.  Meeting clients' needs

Module 36: Eating Right and Light (4 hours)
A.  Reducing fat and calories as part of a healthy diet
B.  Meal planning
C.  Reducing fat in meals
D.  Food selection
E.  Food buying
F.  Food preparation

Module 37: Observation/Practice Teaching with Experienced NPA
(6 hours)
A.  Complete observation of teaching visit forms
B.  Look for
    1.  Teaching techniques
    2.  Recruitment techniques
    3.  NPA relationship with participants
    4.  Time management skills

Unit V—Content Outline

Module 38: Scanning the Territory (6 hours)
A.  Territory assignments
B.  Low-income neighborhoods within territory
C.  Existing referrals
D.  Potential referrals
E.  Division of territory
F.  Preparing program planning sheet

Module 39: On-the-Job Training (6 hours)
Recruit program participants in new territory with
assistance from an experienced NPA.

Module 40: On-the-Job Training (6 hours)
Recruit program participants in new territory with
assistance from an experienced NPA.

Module 41: On-the-Job Training (6 hours)
Recruit program participants in new territory with
assistance from an experienced NPA.

Module 42: Solo Recruitment (6 hours)
A. Recruit Program Participants in New Territory
B. Conference with Supervisor

# REFERENCES

American Society for Training and Development (ASTD). (1990, May). *Info-Line: How to conduct a performance appraisal* (Issue 9005). Alexandria, VA: Author.

Baker, S. S. (1994). *EFNEP program assistant orientation and training program*. Unpublished master's project, North Carolina State University, Raleigh.

Beatty, R. (1995). *The interview kit*. New York: Wiley.

Bridges, W. (1991). *Managing transitions*. Reading, MA: Addison-Wesley.

Brookfield, S. (1986). *Understanding and facilitating adult learning: A comprehensive analysis of principles and effective practices*. San Francisco: Jossey-Bass.

Caine, R., & Caine, G. (1994). *Making connections: Teaching and the human brain*. Menlo Park, CA: Addison-Wesley.

Carnevale, A., Gainer, L., & Meltzer, A. (1990a). *Workplace basics: The essential skills employers want*. San Francisco: Jossey-Bass.

Carnevale, A., Gainer, L., & Meltzer, A. (1990b). *Workplace basics training manual*. San Francisco: Jossey-Bass.

Chesterton, J. (1995). Shattering the myths of hourly workers. *Management Review, 84*(9), 56–60.

Galbraith, M. W., Sisco, B. R., & Guglielmino, L. M. (1997). *Administering successful programs for adults*. Malabar, FL: Krieger.

Gardner, H. (1983). *Frames of mind*. New York: HarperCollins.

Goleman, D. (1995). *Emotional intelligence*. New York: Bantam.

Heyman, R. (1994). *Why didn't you say that in the first place?* San Francisco: Jossey-Bass.

Kistin, N., Abramson, R., & Dublin, P. (1994). Effect of peer counselors on breastfeeding initiation, exclusivity, and duration among low-income women. *Journal of Human Lactation, 10*(1), 11–15.

Knowles, M. (1980). *The modern practice of adult education* (Rev. ed.). Chicago: Follett.

Lazear, D. (1994). *Seven pathways of learning.* Tuscon, AZ: Zephyr Press.

Maddux, R. (1987). *Effective performance appraisals.* (Rev. ed.). Los Altos, CA: Crisp Publications.

Maslow, A. (1968). *Toward a psychology of being.* New York: Littleton Education Publishing.

Mehrens, W. (1989). *Michigan employability skills employer survey.* Technical Report. Lansing, MI: Michigan State University.

Mezirow, J. and Associates. (1990). *Fostering critical reflection in adulthood.* San Francisco: Jossey-Bass.

National Academy of Sciences (NAS). (1984). *High schools and the changing workplace: The employers' view* (NTIS No. PB84-240191). Washington, DC: National Academy Press.

New York State Education Department. (1990). *Basic and expanded basic skills: Scales for validation study.* Albany, NY: Author.

O'Neil, H. F., Allred, K., & Baker, E. L. (1992). *Measurement of workforce readiness: Review of theoretical frameworks* (CAE Technical Report 343). Los Angles, CA: University of California, Center for Research on Evaluation, Standards and Student Testing (CRESST).

Olson, C. (1994). *Review of the research on the effects of training in nutrition education on intermediaries, paraprofessionals and professionals.* Technical paper prepared for the U.S. Department of Agriculture, Food and Consumer Service. Alexandria, VA.

Peoples, D. (1992). *Presentations plus.* New York: Wiley.

Rose, C., & Nicholl, M. (1997). *Accelerated learning for the 21st century.* New York: Delacorte Press.

Silberman, M. (1996). *Active learning: 101 strategies to teach any subject.* Needham Heights, MA: Allyn and Bacon.

Truax, C., & Carkhuff, R. (1967). *Toward effective counseling and psychotherapy.* Chicago: Aldine.

U.S. Department of Labor, The Secretary's Commission on Achieving Necessary Skills (SCANS). (1991). *What work requires of schools: A SCANS report for American 2000.* Washington, DC: Author.

Vella, J. (1994). *Learning to listen, learning to teach.* San Francisco: Jossey-Bass.

Vella, J. (1995). *Training through dialogue.* San Francisco: Jossey-Bass.

Wilder, C. (1994). *The presentations kit.* New York: Wiley.

Wlodkowski, R. (1993). *Enhancing adult motivation to learn.* San Francisco: Jossey-Bass.

# INDEX

## DATE DUE

| | | | |
|---|---|---|---|
| | | | |

GAYLORD

PRINTED IN U.S.A.